Landmarks of wor

Boris Pasternak

DOCTOR ZHIVAGO

Landmarks of world literature

General Editor: J. P. Stern

Dickens: *Bleak House* – Graham Storey
Homer: *The Iliad* – Michael Silk
Dante: *The Divine Comedy* – Robin Kirkpatrick
Rousseau: *Confessions* – Peter France
Goethe: *Faust. Part One* – Nicholas Boyle
Woolf: *The Waves* – Eric Warner
Goethe: *The Sorrows of Young Werther* – Martin Swales
Constant: *Adolphe* – Dennis Wood
Balzac: *Old Goriot* – David Bellos
Mann: *Buddenbrooks* – Hugh Ridley
Homer: *The Odyssey* – Jasper Griffin
Tolstoy: *Anna Karenina* – Anthony Thorlby
Conrad: *Nostromo* – Ian Watt
Camus: *The Stranger* – Patrick McCarthy
Murasaki Shikibu: *The Tale of Genji* – Richard Bowring
Sterne: *Tristram Shandy* – Wolfgang Iser
Shakespeare: *Hamlet* – Paul A. Cantor
Stendhal: *The Red and the Black* – Stirling Haig
Brontë: *Wuthering Heights* – U. C. Knoepflmacher
Pasternak: *Doctor Zhivago* – Angela Livingstone
Proust: *Swann's Way* – Sheila Stern

BORIS PASTERNAK

Doctor Zhivago

ANGELA LIVINGSTONE

University of Essex

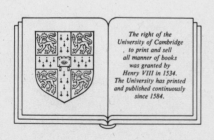

The right of the
University of Cambridge
to print and sell
all manner of books
was granted by
Henry VIII in 1534.
The University has printed
and published continuously
since 1584.

CAMBRIDGE UNIVERSITY PRESS

Cambridge

New York   New Rochelle   Melbourne   Sydney

Published by the Press Syndicate of the University of Cambridge
The Pitt Building, Trumpington Street, Cambridge CB2 1RP
32 East 57th Street, New York, NY 10022, USA
10 Stamford Road, Oakleigh, Melbourne 3166, Australia

© Cambridge University Press 1989

First published 1989

Printed in Great Britain at the University Press, Cambridge

British Library cataloguing in publication data

Livingstone, Angela
Boris Pasternak, Doctor Zhivago. −
(Landmarks of world literature)
1. Fiction in Russian. Pasternak, Boris,
1890–1960
I. Title   II. Series
891.73'42

Library of Congress cataloguing in publication data
Applied for

ISBN 0 521 32811 X hard covers
ISBN 0 521 31698 7 paperback

for Sonia and Benjamin

Contents

Acknowledgements

I wish to thank Diane Fahey for reading this book in typescript and offering valuable comments, Stephen Smith for advising me on Russian history, and Valentina Coe for her ready help with questions of Russian language. Several friends and colleagues helped me with an earlier version of the text: I am grateful to them all and will especially mention the assistance of Evgenii and Elena Pasternak in Moscow. My two visits to them there were financed by the British Council and the British Academy. Another period of work on the book was spent at the Slavic Summer Research Laboratory of the University of Illinois, to whose members I am grateful for their provision of ideal work conditions.

Note

Pasternak divided his novel into two *volumes*, containing altogether seventeen *parts*, each of these being divided into sections. Volume 2 starts at Part 8. Part 17 consists of the twenty-five 'Poems of Yurii Zhivago', and is so entitled. The English translators altered this by dividing the book into two 'parts' containing altogether sixteen 'chapters', followed by the poems as an unnumbered appendix. One American edition (Ballantine Books) diverges still more from the original by making 'Part 2' start at 'chapter 5'. *My references are to Pasternak's own arrangement of the book.*

All quotations are given in my own translation (except in two instances: on pages 74 and 83). This often differs from the published translation. To facilitate finding the place, for most longer quotations and some shorter ones I refer to Part and section. For example, '2:5' means 'Part 2, (section) 5'. In the English translation of the novel, this is 'chapter 2, (section) 5'.

Where I have had to transliterate Russian words, I have used the most common English system, which gives 'х' as 'kh' and 'ч' as 'ch', but I render both 'и' and 'й' as 'i', 'ы' as 'y', and 'е' as 'e' (not 'ye'). In the novel, the main character is called by several variants of his name, but I refer to him mainly as 'Yurii', sometimes as 'Zhivago'. The name of the town which the translators call 'Melyuzeevo' I have corrected to 'Melyuzeev'.

Chronology

Major publications of Pasternak's works are given in italics. They are poetry except where otherwise stated. His translations are not listed in detail.

Pasternak's life and works	*Major literary and historical events*
1881	Death of Dostoevsky.
1886	Chekhov's fame begins.
1889	Birth of Akhmatova.
1890 Born in Moscow. Brother and two sisters born 1893, 1900, 1902.	
1891	Birth of Mandelstam.
1892	Birth of Tsvetaeva.
1893	Birth of Mayakovsky.
1895	Birth of Esenin.
1900 Meets the German poet Rainer Maria Rilke on a train journey.	
1903 Meets the composer Scriabin. Begins a six-year study of composition. Thrown by a horse, breaks his leg, thus 'getting out of two future wars in one evening'.	
1904	Death of Chekhov. Russia's defeat in war with Japan.
1905	Year of revolutionary uprisings and changes.

1906	Spends a year in Germany with his family.	
1908	Enters Moscow University to study law.	
1909	Is encouraged by Scriabin to make his career in music; decides not to. Joins 'Serdarda', a group of young poets, artists and musicians. Becomes student of philosophy.	
1910		Death of Tolstoy.
1911		Assassination of Prime Minister Stolypin.
1912	Studies for a semester at the University of Marburg under Hermann Cohen, who encourages him to make his career in philosophy; decides not to. Visits Italy.	
1913	Graduates from University.	Belyi's novel, *Petersburg*. Mandelstam, *Stone*.
1914	Joins 'Centrifuga', a moderate Futurist group. Meets Mayakovsky. *Twin in the Clouds*.	1914–18, World War I.
1914–16	Works as tutor. Does civilian war service in the Urals.	
1916		Mayakovsky, 'Cloud in Trousers'.
1917	Returns to Moscow. *Above the Barriers*.	February and October Revolutions.
1918		Blok, 'The Twelve'. 1918–20, Civil War.
1921	Parents and sisters emigrate.	Death of Blok. Execution of Gumilyov.

1922	Marries Evgeniya Lurye, an artist; spends seven months with her in Germany. *My Sister Life*.	Mandelstam, *Tristia*. Eliot, 'The Waste Land'; Joyce, *Ulysses*; Rilke, *Duino Elegies*.
1923	Joins neo-Futurist group 'Lef'. Living in poverty but is now a poet of some fame. Birth of son, Evgenii. *Themes and Variations*.	
1924	Works briefly for Commissariat of Education.	Death of Lenin (January). Beginning of Stalin's rise to power.
1925	*Aerial Ways* (4 stories: 'The Stroke of Appelles', 'Letters from Tula', 'The Childhood of Lyuvers', 'Aerial Ways'). *The Year Nineteen Hundred and Five*.	Resolution on Literature published by Communist Party. Suicide of Esenin.
1926	*Lieutenant Schmidt*.	Babel's stories, *Red Cavalry*. Death of Rilke in Switzerland.
1928	*Lofty Malady*.	Inauguration of first Five Year Plan for intensive industrialisation and the collectivisation of agriculture.
1929	*A Tale* (prose).	
1930	Separates from first wife; marries Zinaida Neigaus, a musician; their first stay in Georgia.	Suicide of Mayakovsky.
1931	Criticised by RAPP for 'bourgeois idealism'. *A Safe Conduct* (prose autobiography); *Spektorsky* (novel in verse).	
1932	Refuses to sign collective letter writers send Stalin on death of his wife, adds idiosyncratic postscript. *Second Birth*.	Union of Soviet Writers founded.

1933	Begins devoting most of his time to translation, publishing no original work for eleven years.	
1934	Is telephoned by Stalin: in vain Pasternak suggests they should meet to discuss 'life and death'. Speaks at the congress.	First congress of Soviet Writers' Union
1935	Insomnia and depression. Attends Congress of Writers in Defence of Culture, in Paris.	
1936	Is allotted a *dacha* (country house) in Peredelkino, writers' village outside Moscow. Speaks at Writers' Union session in Minsk. Refuses to sign letter condemning generals accused of conspiracy.	1936–38, period of terror, the 'Purge'.
1937	Birth of son, Leonid.	
1938		Death of Mandelstam in a prison camp.
1939	Death of mother in London.	
1940	Translates *Hamlet*.	
1941	Evacuated, with other writers to Chistopol in the Urals: Begins eight years of translating Shakespeare's tragedies.	Suicide of Tsvetaeva. German invasion of U.S.S.R.
1943	Visits the war front. *On Early Trains*.	Battle of Stalingrad.
1945	Death of father in Oxford. *Earth's Expanse*. No new work published until 1954. Begins writing *Doctor Zhivago*.	Soviet troops enter Berlin. End of World War II

1946	Refuses to attend meeting condemning writers Akhmatova and Zoshchenko. Is attacked by Fadeev, Secretary of Writers' Union. Has a growing reputation abroad. Begins fourteen-year love relationship with Olga Ivinskaya.	1946–51, the repressive 'Zhdanov period' in the arts.
1947–49	Further threatening attacks on him by Writers' Union.	
1947–51	Translates Goethe's *Faust* (both parts).	
1949	Supports family of Ivinskaya who is sent to prison because of him (released in 1953). *William Shakespeare in Boris Pasternak's Translation* (translated plays).	
1952	Serious heart attack.	
1953		Death of Stalin.
1956	'Novyi mir' publishers reject *Doctor Zhivago.* Signs contract with State Publishing House for an abridged version and makes agreement with Italian publisher Feltrinelli.	20th congress of the Communist Party: Khrushchev denounces Stalin. 'Thaw' begins in literature. Suicide of Fadeev.
1957	Months in hospital. Publication of the novel is forbidden in the Soviet Union. In November Feltrinelli publishes it in Italian translation. *Doctor Zhivago.*	

1958	Again ill. Is awarded the Nobel Prize for Literature. *Doctor Zhivago* is translated and published in many countries. Pasternak is expelled from the Writers' Union, and has to renounce the Prize. *Autobiographical Sketch* (prose, published abroad).
1959	*When the Weather Clears* (published abroad). Feltrinelli publishes *Doctor Zhivago* in Russian.
1960	Dies, of lung cancer. Several thousand people attend his funeral in Peredelkino. *The Blind Beauty* (incomplete play, published abroad).
1965	Film *Doctor Zhivago* is made in California.
1966	Death of Akhmatova, the last great poet with spiritual roots in the pre-revolutionary time. Bulgakov's novel, *The Master and Margarita*.
1970	Award of the Nobel Prize to Solzhenitsyn.
1974	Expulsion of Solzhenitsyn from the Soviet Union.
1985	Gorbachev becomes First Secretary of the Communist Party. Subsequently, in the atmosphere of 'glasnost', numerous hitherto prohibited literary works are published.
1988	*Doctor Zhivago* is serialized in the journal *Novyi mir* – its first publication in the Soviet Union. A five-volume edition of Pasternak's collected works is announced for 1989.

Chapter 1

Reception, importance and position of *Doctor Zhivago*

I would pretend to have seen nature and universe themselves not as a picture made or fastened on an immoveable wall but as a sort of painted canvas roof or curtain in the air, incessantly pulled and blown and flapped by a something of an immaterial unknown and unknowable wind.

This sentence comes from a letter Pasternak wrote in 1959. He was writing in English, so there are some oddities of expression: by 'pretend' he may mean 'claim'. It describes what he would do to get art to resemble 'living reality'. Rather than seek to convey any particular thing or state of affairs, he would write, he says, as if he had seen everything at once – 'nature and universe themselves'; moreover, as if he had seen it all in endless, mysterious movement. This is what he set out to do in *Doctor Zhivago*.

The extraordinary metaphor of the painted canvas blowing in the wind points to the heart of Pasternak's work. We shall come back to it, or to what it implies, more than once, as indeed he himself kept coming back to it. Later in this introductory chapter I shall relate it more closely to *Doctor Zhivago*. But first I propose to consider Pasternak's novel in its time and place, asking how it was received and what makes it a 'landmark'.

In 1958, people started talking about Pasternak all over the world. Journalists, literary critics, people in public life, writers and readers, all suddenly became interested in this Russian who had written a novel which his own country refused to publish even though he had been appreciated as a poet there for some forty years. Its publication abroad was rapidly followed by his being honoured with the highest international award for literature, the Nobel Prize.

Pasternak never sought fame, but the book made him famous and the Prize made him more so. The violent reaction of the Soviet authorities made him more famous still. *Doctor Zhivago* was denounced as an anti-Soviet work by large numbers of Soviet citizens who had not read it. Its author was attacked as a traitor and condemned in the Press and at writers' meetings in the most vituperative language: he was not merely a 'literary weed' but a 'pig fouling its own den', a 'snake enjoying the odour of decay in poetical dung-waters of lyrical manure', a 'mangy sheep' and various other animals. But name-calling was the least of it. Pasternak was expelled from the Writers' Union — the sole means by which Soviet writers can publish and prosper — and threatened with exile and deprivation of citizenship. The international PEN Club and influential individuals in other countries tried to intercede with the Soviet powers but it was not until he had written two public letters acknowledging 'mistakes' and asking to be allowed to stay in Russia that he was left in peace — under close surveillance. Only in 1988, more than thirty years after its world-wide publication, has Pasternak's novel appeared in its own country. Though his other works were reprinted, *Doctor Zhivago* could not even be mentioned before the intellectual liberalisation now introduced by Mikhail Gorbachev.

While persecuted by his fellow-countrymen, Pasternak found himself winning friends in the rest of the world, receiving up to seventy foreign letters a day, most of which expressed admiration. Except at home, people were writing about him everywhere. By the end of 1959, some 350 articles had appeared, acclaiming *Doctor Zhivago* as a great work of art or a great statement, or, at the very least, a great event. As N. Chiaromonte wrote: 'Here is Russia, once again speaking out freely'.

If a landmark is 'a conspicuous object in the landscape which serves as a guide', the furore over *Doctor Zhivago* undoubtedly made it a landmark in literary history. How conspicuous would it have been without the furore? How clearly does it stand out now, thirty years afterwards? And to what is it a guide?

It certainly stands out as a large novel about large subjects. We encounter in it a quarter of a century of tremendous historical change: the 1905 revolution, the First World War, the two revolutions of 1917, the Civil War, and the subsequent decade of social, economic, political and personal transformation in Russia. Its depiction of an important period of history reflected in individual lives has made some readers compare it to Tolstoy's *War and Peace*.

It stands out too for its discussion of large human questions: what is history? what is art? what do we live for? do we need religion? what is existence all about? These Tolstoyan questions and Pasternak's answers to them are explicit or implicit throughout the book and lead some to call it a philosophical novel.

To Pasternak himself it was a supreme landmark, an infinitely greater achievement than anything else in his achievement-filled life. He had not previously been known for making long lucid statements; more often he seemed an inspired stammerer or a lyrical spirit unable (as he said) to ward off 'the slanting images flying in a downpour' through his window and onto the page of his notebook. Now, in his one and only novel, which he referred to as his 'novel in prose', he had made for the first time a large general statement in familiar language.

Russians who read the book clandestinely saw it as a landmark both in Pasternak's work and in the censorship-ridden culture they had become used to in the preceding three decades. Free and outspoken, it conveyed an authentic personal experience of the Revolution with little regard for the restraints that made most writers either 'toe the Party line' or 'write for the desk drawer'. It sympathetically evoked the atmosphere of pre-revolutionary Russian culture. It was a defence of poetry. And it spoke warmly of religion, for some even becoming a guide to the religious life. 'A miracle of nonconformity', said Victor Frank, a Russian scholar living in the west, 'full of supreme indifference to all the official taboos'.

Meanwhile many of the book's non-Russian readers

experienced it as renewing that youthful zest for living which the translation of nineteenth-century Russian novels at the beginning of this century had seemed to bring into the ageing culture of Europe — the same unsophisticated critical attitude and unashamed concern with spirituality. Like those earlier novels, it was also praised because, contrary to the 'microscopic analyses of western novelists', it was (to quote Czeslaw Milosz) 'open to huge vistas of space and historical time'. It was a guide to simple-heartedness and to a rediscovery of the eternal values: love, beauty, art, faith. It was like the best of the past returned. Readers compared its hero not only to the Holy Fool of Orthodox tradition and the 'superfluous man' of the Russian nineteenth-century novel, but also to Odysseus, Everyman, Hamlet, Faust and Jesus Christ.

I hope to show that *Doctor Zhivago* is more than a work of conservation or restoration, that it offers something unique, not easy to sum up, through which it is a landmark of another kind and a guide to something less nameable than 'religion' or 'personality' or 'perennial human values'. Motifs of waking up and of resurrection are woven throughout the book. A nightingale's song is described as 'falling into two syllables, summoning, heartfelt, imploring, resembling a plea or an admonition: wake up! wake up! wake up!' (the translators curtailed this important passage), and each of the hero's bouts of illness and recovery is presented as a dream-descent into Hell and a waking up to Heaven. Several commentators have discussed the resurrection imagery. But what is it Yurii wakes or is resurrected *to*? What was Pasternak hoping everyone who read this book would wake to see?

It is evident that waking up includes starting to live without pretentiousness and verbiage. Such change was a lifelong preoccupation of Pasternak's. In 1932 he wrote, in a love poem: 'It's easy to wake up and start to see, / to shake the wordy rubbish from one's heart / and live not getting cluttered any more — / all this is no great cunning.' What is seen, then, when the clutter is gone? I believe an answer is given in every aspect of the novel, which could thus be called a book with a message, even with a mission. Not, though, with a definitely worked out ideological system. In her excellent essay on *Zhivago* written shortly after its publication, Helen Muchnic wrote that in it 'Religion, politics, philosophical discourses are peripheral to a prevailing sense of wonder', and this goes some way towards summing up Pasternak's message.

Critics have had trouble describing the form of *Doctor Zhivago* and even the genre it belongs to. *Is* it a novel? many have asked. Isn't it too lyrical, subjective, shapeless, to be called that? There are long diary entries in it, its dialogues are virtually monologues, its landscapes and described states of mind can be lifted out and read on their own, almost as poems, and its last chapter actually consists of poems: Isn't the whole thing some kind of poem? It has been called 'a rhapsody', 'a kind of morality play', 'an introspective epic', 'a poet's novel', 'an apocalyptic poem in the form of a novel', yet also 'a political novel par excellence', 'a love story for all time', as well as 'one of the most original works of modern times', 'something wholly *sui generis*', and 'one of the most paradoxical phenomena in twentieth-century European culture'. Perhaps what Tolstoy said about *War and Peace* should be said about *Doctor Zhivago*: it was 'what the author wanted to express, and was able to express, in the form in which it was expressed'.

There have been disagreements as to which century *Doctor Zhivago* really belongs to. Some find it modern, even 'modernist', others find it old fashioned, 'a nineteenth-century novel by a twentieth-century poet'. What does link it with the literary traditions of the nineteenth century is its concern for the fate of Russia. Russian literature, after springing miraculously into existence with Pushkin (1799–1837) and fountaining into a half-century of writers of genius, has always had an exceptional real-life importance to its writers and readers. It was never thought of as mere self-expression, embellishment of experience or entertainment, but always as a most serious part of living, the expression of an active understanding of society and an interpretation of Russia's role in the world. It was highly conscious of its Russianness. With the dark ages only just behind them and the 'dark folk' all around them, and with vital social and philosophical questions still unsolved and urgent, writers in Russia often took on a special responsibility as moral guides, explorers and discoverers. Literature became a kind of parliament, a means of freely discussing society and the human condition, other forms of utterance being lamed by censorship, persecution, and the absence of usable institutions. Dostoevsky's novels plunge into questions of good and evil, Heaven and Hell, freedom and despotism; and in Tolstoy's the existence of God, the moral status of art, the nature of history and the iniquities of the social system often loom as large as do the characters and story. So Pasternak becomes another notable instance of the Russian writer taking on public moral responsibility when even he, poet of gardens and weathers, singer of love and of language, finally steps on to the public stage to record history, judge society, debate and define the nature of human being.

Nonetheless *Doctor Zhivago* is very different from the Russian and European novels of the nineteenth century with their consequential plot lines, interest in motivation and construction of rounded characters. One could never say of Pasternak's characters, as readers often claim of Tolstoy's, that one feels one has really met them, nor (as Bakhtin has shown of Dostoevsky's) that each one speaks from a separate and unique centre of consciousness. On the contrary, they tend to merge, overlap and add up to a single mind. Pasternak deliberately set out to oppose the realist tradition. In the letter to the English poet Stephen Spender from which our opening quotation comes — printed in *Encounter* for August 1960 — he mentions the 'not sufficient tracing of characters I was reproached with' and adds (in brackets): 'more than to delineate them I tried to efface them'.

The short correspondence with Spender, which Pasternak conducted in English, contains illuminating remarks about what he was attempting in his novel. In all great creative works, he writes, there is 'a characterisation of reality as such' and the nineteenth-century way of characterising it was to apply 'the incontestable doctrine of causality, the belief . . . that all appearances of the moral and material world were subordinate to the law of sequels and retributions . . . The tragic bewitching spell of Flaubert's style or Maupassant's manner roots in the fact that their narratives are irrevocable like verdicts or sentences.' He adds that he too sought to characterise reality as such, for he had always been 'struck by the observation that existence was more original, extraordinary and inexplicable than any of its separate astonishing incidents and facts. I was attracted by the unusualness of the usual.' This is typical of Pasternak: creativity starts from astonishment at the way things are. As a writer he was happiest when he had 'succeeded in rendering *the atmosphere of being*' – which was no longer made up of causality and inevitability.

It is remarkable that Pasternak says nothing about twentieth-century innovations in the novel form. The literary models he takes as his point of departure are all earlier ones, and he talks as if he were the sole writer in dialogue with them. A journalist who visited him in 1957 reported that he spoke of Goethe and Shakespeare as if they were his contemporaries. He seems to have felt sure that no one else was doing what he was doing.

In the same letter Pasternak explains what constituted the new 'atmosphere':

There is an effort in the novel to represent the whole sequence of facts and beings and happenings like some moving entireness, like a developing, passing by, rolling and rushing inspiration, as if reality itself had freedom and choice and was composing itself out of numberless variants and versions.

This echoes a whole series of assertions within the novel. I shall quote two of them, one near the beginning, one near the end. Yurii consoles a sick woman, saying that though there can be no physical resurrection in any future world, 'all the while, one and the same immensely identical life fills the universe and is renewed hour by hour in innumerable combinations and transformations' (3:3). And later he objects to Bolshevik ideas of mechanically remaking everything:

The re-making of life! Those who talk in this way . . . have not once come to know life, not felt its spirit, its soul . . . Life is never a material, a substance. If you want to know, it is an uninterruptedly self-renewing, eternally self-working principle, it eternally re-makes and refashions itself, it itself is infinitely grander than the obtuse theories held by you or me.   (11:5)

This thought is the novel's philosophical basis, its 'vitalism', as Guy de Mallac calls it. Zhivago himself puts it forward more as a passionate feeling than as an idea. Meanwhile the epigrammatic phrases of his philosopher-uncle, Vedenyapin — 'life is meaningful because it is symbolical', 'communion between mortals is immortal' — underpin the idea by implying a view of existence as meaning something 'tangibly more than itself'.

Several attempts have been made, or initiated, to interpret images, names and references throughout *Zhivago* as belonging to a consistent symbolic system. The most thoroughgoing is that of M. F. and P. Rowland who, with the help of Greek and Oriental mythology, the Bible, the work of Jung, Siberian shamanism and old Russian epic, identify allegory at every step and produce a fascinating view of the novel as concerned with the soul's descent into Hell and its salvation: fascinating, but over-inventive, and complicated in ways that Pasternak both implicitly and explicitly avoided. Their categorising of *Doctor Zhivago* as 'symbolic realism' seems to me apt, neatly linking its two aspects. But their method neglects the meanings the novel can offer to a non-scholarly, impressionistic reading, and pays close attention only to selected features, so that the overall pattern of the work is scarcely noticed. I shall give a more flexible reading and shall not pursue any such detailed allegory as that Anna Gromeko 'represents doomed Imperial Russia', and Yurii's mother — the Russian Church, or even that Lara is 'the quintessential spirit of Russia', although Yurii does sometimes think of her in this way.

Not that I do not think every detail has its meaning; nearly every name, for example, will yield to at least one interpretation. But I believe we should heed Pasternak's warning that if readers get too enthusiastic in hunting down the significances of details they miss the sense of the whole work. His image of the painted canvas, quoted at the beginning of this chapter, suggests the proper relation of parts to whole. For, as other instances of the same image make clear, he had in mind a canvas with a picture painted on it. The details of the picture represent the features of the real world and — when the picture is motionless — those of the realist novel. Far more interesting than these is the fact that the entire picture, the canvas itself, is in movement, blown and flapped by a wind coming from elsewhere.

There are many descriptions of movement within the novel, but all of them at once (as in the poem 'Wind', 'all the trees as one entirety') are seen as moving under the influence of a force from outside. There is no need to say what that is. Pasternak is not looking for transcendental definitions. All his effort is devoted to evoking the moving historical and seasonal world as he experiences it — the painting blowing in an infinite wind. One way of reading *Zhivago*, then, is to see it as built up on praise for, and delight in, movement, process, change, life's energy and dynamism, and, accompanying this, on incredulity and horror at their opposite: fixity, entropy, the tendency to put a stop to movement and turn process into stasis, the unadmitted will to death and deadliness.

The symbolic dimension, along with the indifference, at times hostility, expressed in it towards politics and Marxist ideology, make *Doctor Zhivago* far removed from socialist realism, that ill-defined but restrictive model set up for literature in the Soviet Union from 1932 onwards. The first part of its demand — literature must 'represent reality in its revolutionary development' — might be seen as answered by Pasternak if one took 'revolutionary' to mean dynamic and changing, but the second part could not: writers must take on the 'task of ideological transformation and education of the workers in the spirit of socialism'. According to socialist realism, literature had to be socially useful, present 'positive heroes' and express optimism; novels were to imitate Tolstoy in being realistic, non-experimental and easy to read; writers were to be 'party-minded' (as Lenin said back in 1905: 'Down with non-party-minded writers! Down with the literary supermen!'). The mechanistic rhetoric Pasternak deplores was often heard in the later 1920s and 30s: writers were 'engineers of human souls', their work was to be 'cog and screw' of the social machine, they would 'sow the iron seed' of Bolshevism, help reconstruct the world. Novels began to have such titles as *The Iron Flood*, *Cement*, *How the Steel was Tempered*, or *The Story of a Real Man*, *The Making of a Hero*. Successful plots were about the building of a hydroelectric power plant or how a soldier, such as Levinson in Fadeev's *Rout*, masterfully crumples the love-letter in his pocket and sacrifices himself to serve an abstract cause.

When the *Novyi mir* editors wrote to Pasternak explaining why they would not publish his novel, they had socialist realist principles in mind. Pasternak had not yet become anathema to the authorities (this was before the Nobel Prize award) and their long letter is a courteous enough document, notwithstanding its sneers at 'truth-seeking individuals' and its patronising confidence of knowing his book better than he did. They considered its spirit to be simply 'non-acceptance of the socialist revolution'. They saw Zhivago as a pleasure-loving egotist angry with the revolution for destroying his physical comforts, a cowardly evader of the all-important question, 'Whose side are you on?', who does not even distinguish the February (bourgeois) revolution from the October (socialist) one. Yet it is easy enough to show that Zhivago does not value material comforts, and we shall be discussing his changing responses to the events of 1917. Other and various views of the book's attitude to the Revolution have been taken by western readers, some saying it treats it 'as a malady', others that it represents it as 'one of the few great events of human history', Vladimir Nabokov calling it 'pro-Bolshevist', and Frank O'Hara giving this interesting analysis: 'if Pasternak is saying the 1917 Revolution failed, he must have felt that the West never even made the attempt.

Far from being a traitorous work [*Zhivago*] is a poem on the nobility of the Soviet failure to reconstruct society *in human terms*, and it is not without hope.' But perhaps the *Novyi mir* editors' chief blindness was their failure to see that the book is not centrally about politics at all, or even about personalities, but is about creativity, understood as an energy and an integral part of human life and history.

Except in talent, novelty and refusal to be scared of the censor, *Doctor Zhivago* has little in common with other outstanding fictional works of the post-revolutionary period. Babel's cycle of stories known in English as *Red Cavalry* (published in 1926 but attacked for not giving a correct view of the Communist Party) is about the Civil War and the 'heart-gratings' of an intellectual amongst men of action. Platonov's grippingly melancholy novel *The Foundation Pit* (written in the thirties but not published in the Soviet Union until 1987, and still undervalued in the west) is set among the brutalities of the collectivisation of agriculture. Zamyatin's *We* (published abroad in 1924 but not published in Russia until 1988) depicts an anti-Utopia in which people are 'numbers', 'personal life' is limited to an hour a day, and all imagination is finally removed by surgery. Bulgakov's *Master and Margarita* (published only in 1966, thirty years after it was written) combines New Testament reality with a fantasy-satire on modern Moscow, with the Devil as one of its characters. From all these, *Zhivago* differs both in its celebratory spirit and in its attempt at a straightforward style, a new realism. The other writers mentioned are concerned with innovation in literary language or in ways of projecting the authorial voice, but Pasternak, like his hero, sought 'an originality that would be concealed under a cover of commonplace and familiar forms, a restrained, unpretentious . . . unnoticeable style that would attract no one's attention'.

In these respects he also stands aside from the major European fiction writers of our time. There is nothing in him of the refined, self-conscious narratorial poise of Thomas Mann or Proust, of Joyce or Virginia Woolf, the works of all of whom he had read, although, as he knew, most of his hoped-for Soviet readers would not have done so.

Eric Warner writes of Virginia Woolf's *The Waves* that it 'deliberately strives for the palm of innovation so assiduously courted by modernist art' and 'there remains something unsettling in its dazzling display of technique, something which . . . renders the book overly enigmatic and elusive'. Words like these were often applied to Pasternak's earlier writings too, but by the time of *Zhivago* he was striving for just the contrary of the palm of innovation. Dazzling technique came easily to him and needed no striving for. Simple communication came with difficulty and almost as a heroic exploit. *Doctor Zhivago* is the attained goal of a lifelong journey. Does this mean one needs to know the earlier works in order to appreciate it? Of course the novel must stand on its own and be judged for what it is, yet some acquaintance with the earlier writings helps to understand the personal achievement. It could even suggest a biographic subtext to the many attacks (by Yurii and Lara and the implied author) on the verbiage, cliché-mania and rhetoric so widespread in the Communist period: in repudiating all that, Pasternak was perhaps also dissociating himself from his own previous sins of wordiness. Not that he had ever practised empty verbiage − his sin (if it was one) had been the opposite: never a cliché to be seen! every image vibrant with originality − but still a *lot* of words. His search for an unnoticeable style was a reaction not only to the over-noticeable style of the age but also to his own youthful abundances. To read some of his pre-1940 works − which he once said he would not lift a finger to save from oblivion − is to come back to *Zhivago* with a keen awareness of the difficulty Pasternak had in not being difficult. And this, at the very least, may make us forgive and perhaps overlook the occasional ineptly written passages: they are the stumblings not of someone who cannot walk, but of someone more accustomed to acrobatics and dance. With a few exceptions I am not going to refer to his earlier poetry, since this loses so much in translation, but I will give, in chapters 2 and 3, some account of the earlier prose works, all of which are now available in acceptable English versions.

Several Russian writers are mentioned in *Doctor Zhivago*, most notably Pushkin, Tolstoy and Alexander Blok. Outside the book, Pasternak spoke of his admiration for Joyce, Proust and Mann. But the only writer he points to as a really important influence on him is the poet Rainer Maria Rilke. His whole personality, he said, had been created by Rilke, and at the end of his life he wrote that he had never, all his life long, done anything other than 'translate' Rilke and 'sail in his waters'. It is not obvious how this applies to *Zhivago*, though Pasternak once described his novel as 'the world of Malte Laurids Brigge' (Rilke's novel of 1910), and once, during the writing of it, he jotted down an instruction to himself 'to set things out peacefully and naturally, like the impression got from re-reading Malte Laurids Brigge'. Yet *Malte* has none of the spaciousness of *Zhivago*, and its defining emotions are a finely analysed fear and horror, while *Zhivago*'s are a boldly asserted joy and affirmation. So their affinity may lie in the fact that both are meditations on what it is like to be a poet in an unpoetic time. As well as this, both seem to possess, for many readers, an indefinable attraction and power. When Pasternak sent a draft of part of his novel, in 1948, to his scholarly, responsive cousin Olga Freidenberg, she wrote to him that she was trying to define her judgment of it:

I'm at a loss: what is my judgement of life? This is life − in the widest and biggest sense . . . What emanates from it is something enormous. Its peculiarity is somehow special (an unintended tautology) and it isn't in the genre or the plot − I can't define it . . . it is a special version of the Book of Genesis . . . Realism of genre and language doesn't interest me. That's not what I value. In the novel there is a grandeur of another kind.

Chapter 2

Pasternak's life, work and times up to 1917

Yurii Zhivago thinks his author's thoughts and writes his poems, but is unlike him in being an orphan, a doctor and not Jewish. In constructing his hero, Pasternak may have been making room for experiences which his actual circumstances excluded – to solitariness, inherited Christianity and a practical vocation. He patently did not regret, however, having the parents he had, being a Jew or living the life of a writer.

Pasternak was born into the most cultured and creative part of the Russian intelligentsia. The art and knowledge of the day were as available to him as food and air. His mother was a celebrated concert pianist, his father a highly successful painter. The best known artists and composers of the time, poets (including Rilke) and scientists (including Einstein), came to their house as friends and to have their portraits painted.

In chapter 1 of his *Autobiographical Sketch*, Pasternak gives two vivid recollections from his childhood, one concerning each parent and both connected with the origin of his creative work. The first – his first conscious memory – is of a night when at four years old he was woken up by music (the novel's 'wake up' motif may derive from this): his mother and two other musicians were playing a trio. To the child it sounded 'disturbing, like real cries for help and news of a disaster coming in from outside the window'. Ever afterward, Pasternak was to think of art as coming 'in through the window': from the real outdoors, not from within the mind; and 'cries for help' occur repeatedly in his accounts of art. Thus in *Doctor Zhivago* Yurii's first glimpse of Lara, an important originating moment in his becoming a poet, makes him aware of a force which he describes as 'dreamlike . . . complaining and calling for help'. Thus the motherly music of sixty years before echoed through to the very end of his writing life.

A few years after this early experience, his father was illustrating Tolstoy's novel *Resurrection* (*Doctor Zhivago*'s resurrection imagery may stem in part from this) – it was being serialised and the drawings were done in a race against time. The chapter, headed 'Infancy', ends with these words, matter-of-fact but clearly describing a glorious pleasure:

On the stove, joiner's glue was boiling. The drawings were hurriedly wiped, dried with fixative, glued to cardboard, wrapped, tied up. The finished parcels were sealed with sealing-wax and handed over to the conductor.

In fact they were handed to a uniformed conductor from the railways who came right into their kitchen to fetch them. The excitement of railways would pervade Pasternak's work and he was always to think of the urgency and happy speed of his father at work as inherent in artistic activity. Art was an exhilaration, a headlong run, a sudden seizure or breathtaking change revealing ordinary things as extraordinary, it was the 'rolling and rushing inspiration' which he wrote to Stephen Spender about, it was the wind blowing the canvas in the sky. Pasternak was spellbound by journeys and preparations for them, as well as by storms, downpours and the tempestuous first moments of revolutions. The best of art was like this for him and the best of life too, and what he loved most in people was any wholeness of gesture and bearing which seemed evidence of their being carried along by a powerful force, like a skater after an 'amazing initial run', as he said both of the poet Mayakovsky and, using almost the same words, of Lara in the novel. Something like that fatherly effortless speed was what he sought in all his writing.

The restrictions relating to Jews in Russia in the nineteenth century were severe, and Pasternak must have witnessed a good deal of prejudice and cruelty. He himself had to put off entering secondary school for a year because the 3 percent quota for Jewish pupils was filled. But the family were largely exempt from the discriminations through his father's having a university degree, and doubtless too through his eminence as an artist. In an unproblematic way, and in several stages, Boris became a Christian. His parents rarely went to the synagogue, and it was no problem to anyone when his Christian nanny baptised him and took him along to Orthodox church services — an overpowering experience of ritual, pageantry, music, incense, emotion. The semi-secret baptism meant for the boy 'a rare exceptional inspiration'. Then there were a few years in his early twenties when he lived, he said, 'largely in a Christian frame of mind'. Later still, in the Second World War, after a horrific night of fire watching and air raids, he was deeply moved by re-reading the New Testament (the *Doctor Zhivago* poem 'Dawn' refers to this). Some Orthodox theologians have found Pasternak's views eccentric. But the Cistercian monk Thomas Merton called him a primitive Christian, 'a naturally Christian spirit'. It seems that the 'rare' quality Christianity had for him in childhood and the inspiration it was for him on the two later occasions were due to his coming to it from the outside. At the same time the ease of the transition, and the pleasure of seeing that, though a Jew, he was so easily at home in Christendom, must have led to his writing about the Jews in *Zhivago* with an assured simplicity that has offended some Jewish readers. He writes as if there were only one view of the matter: 'Don't bunch together', he has the converted Jew Misha Gordon say to Jews generally, 'disperse. Be with everyone. You are the first and best Christians of the world.' Here Pasternak clearly intends Christianity to stand for universality and for the belief that personality is more to be valued than party or faction, nation or race.

When four-year-old Boris woke in the night, one of the guests he glimpsed was a small old man whose spirit filled their household: Lev Tolstoy. If the mixture of rapture and gravity infusing Pasternak's work owes something to the influence of

Rilke, his driving desire for honesty, for an unpretentious and unspectacular way of being original, must be linked to the influence upon him, from earliest childhood, of Tolstoy — the novelist, moralist and propounder of a simplified Christian religion, to whom admirers and disciples were flocking in the 1890s from all quarters of the globe. In 1910 Pasternak accompanied his father to the rural railway station in Tula province where Tolstoy had just died. Always alert to the odd crossings and interweavings of things, he noticed how the sunshine coming in from outside marked the body with the window's cruciform shadow, as well as with little cross-shapes from fir trees. It would seem that this memory lies behind the description of two deaths at the opening of *Doctor Zhivago*, those of Yurii's parents. The priest throws earth onto the body of his mother 'in the shape of a cross'; the blood mark on his dead father's face 'seemed to cross him out' and to be separate from him like mud or a leaf (or — a window shadow?). Since nothing at all is said about Yurii's parents that could connect them with Pasternak's own parents, much may be speculated about Tolstoy as the symbolical father and mother of his novel.

The candlelight, music, suffering and lyricism, in the midst of which Tolstoy was first glimpsed, were one moment in the intensely artistic atmosphere of hard work and high standards in which Pasternak spent his earliest years. He felt destined to be a musician and for six years he studied under a well-known composer. His compositions show the influence of Scriabin, whom he worshipped. Scriabin has been called a Russian reincarnation of Chopin, a 'winged soul, a boundless dreamer'; his trance-like performances at the piano were at once lyrical and grandiose. Pasternak described his music as 'the first settlement of man in the world that Wagner had opened up for chimeras and mastodons', and said he sensed in it 'a staggering naturalness' and overwhelming likeness to modern life. Words like 'staggering' and 'overwhelming' are frequent in his accounts of his youth. Continually uplifted by art and always encountering the best of it, he seems to have had an adolescence in which there was no room whatever for boredom, pettiness or mediocrity.

Round this active and cultured family lay the city of Moscow, which was to be the geographic focus of Pasternak's novel: twice Yurii travels unwillingly away from and gladly back to Moscow, and the very last paragraph calls Moscow the book's real 'heroine', even though so much of its action is elsewhere.

Moscow had been replaced as the capital in 1712 by the new northern city of Petersburg (it would become the capital again in 1918) but it was felt to be the true heart of Russia, its ancient Kremlin being the traditional seat of the tsars and its 'forty times forty' churches the centre of Orthodox Christianity. For Pasternak, in the 1890s Moscow 'still had the look of a remote provincial town as picturesque as in a fairytale', colourful with markets and golden domes, tolling its many bells, having its horses blessed by the church in autumn and closing its post office once a year for a ceremonial visitation by the icon of the post office's patron saint. In winter the snow was shovelled deeply and evenly over the streets and there were magical sleigh rides over the 'moonblue snow', as Pasternak's brother Alexander recalls in his memoir, and as Pasternak himself recalls when he describes the journey of Gromeko and the two boys to the Guichards' sordid hotel.

Sordid things were close by in reality. The Pasternaks lived at the edge of Moscow's grimmest district, full of prostitution and poverty. Pasternak often mentions pity for women as one of his most overpowering feelings in childhood; it is the theme of his story 'A Tale' and in *Zhivago* it is embodied in both Yurii and Strelnikov in their different responses to the corrupted girlhood of Lara.

Political reality too was close at hand and, though he was to say that his intellectual circle was 'apolitical', Pasternak was much affected by politically motivated incidents and by the general expectation of a violent national fate. The chief events of 1905 took place in Petersburg — from Bloody Sunday in January, when peaceful crowds with petitions to the tsar were fired on by the tsar's army, up to the issuing of the October Manifesto, which brought in Russia's first constitution and first parliament. But Moscow felt, just as much as Petersburg did, the turmoil of mutinies, murders, pogroms, strikes and demonstrations, throughout that year. In February the Grand Duke, who was patron of the School of Art in which the Pasternaks lived, was assassinated; after the October Manifesto, which had satisfied only the liberals, the school was equipped with hose-pipes and stones to repel attacks from street crowds. Sixteen-year-old Boris joined in one of the street demonstrations and got struck by the whips of the dragoons who 'cantered off leaving a few bodies on the road', as Alexander Pasternak records it and as we find echoed in the account of that October in *Zhivago*, though the boyish participant here is Pasha Antipov and the dragoon's whip lands on the back of the widow Tiverzin. In December came the armed uprising of workers that made Moscow's Presnya district famous — this too is mentioned in the novel.

The 1905 troubles amounted to the worst crisis yet in the oppressive tsarist regime, and made still more intolerable the enormous gulf between the gentry and the peasants or half-peasant urban workers (many of them serfs before the 1861 liberation). The intelligentsia, although secure in its relation to European cultural traditions, was an endangered and isolated group, alienated from the rigid bureaucratic state on the one hand and, on the other, knowing itself to be a frail stratum of refinement and privilege above the enormous illiterate mass of the Russian people. Very many felt guilt-stricken, many hoped and even worked for fundamental change, while realising it would mean the destruction of their own class and culture. The poet Alexander Blok, whose spirit is invoked more than once in *Doctor Zhivago*, was a tragic and eloquent representative of this attitude.

It was a time of manifold renaissance in Russian culture, with new talent coming to the fore in all the arts. In poetry the Symbolist movement was waning, but new movements waxed, notably Acmeism (praising earthly things, as against the ethereality of the Symbolists) and Futurism (glamorous and rebellious and hoping to throw Pushkin, Tolstoy and most others 'off the ship of modernity'). New publishing ventures sprang up, the visual arts flourished as never before, with exhibitions of foreign and native work – Matisse and Rodin, Malevich and Larionov; Diagilev was making the Russian ballet famous abroad. Russia's cultural development, soon to become isolated from the rest of Europe's, was in the first decade and a half of the century closely interrelated with it. The Russian Symbolists were inspired by the French, the Acmeists had much in common with Anglo-American imagism, the Futurists offered a parallel to the Italian movement of the same name. The two chapters of *A Safe Conduct* (Pasternak's first autobiography) describing that period are rounded off with references to ancient Greece as a natural source of inspiration, and we find the young Pasternak discussing Hegel and Leibniz in the 'Café grec' before setting off to study neo-Kantian philosophy in the German university of Marburg; thence he went to Italy, where he experienced 'the sensation of the palpable unity of our culture'. The sense of belonging to a wider unity, a culture without frontiers, with a shared certainty about what was valuable, was of the first importance to Pasternak and to his novel. It is in contrast to this that he laments the 'herd spirit' and the forming of separate artists' groups with programmes and doctrines. Of labels like 'Symbolist', 'Acmeist', 'Futurist', Pasternak once exclaimed: 'What murderous jargon! Clearly aesthetics is a science which classifies air balloons according to the holes in them which prevent them from flying.'

What made great art, Pasternak believed, was never allegiance to group or principle, but the experience of love, admiration and worship. Indeed, this was what made humanity: 'We have all become people in proportion as we have loved and have had occasion to love.' The story of how he gave up philosophy and devoted himself to poetry is a story of being changed through love – or, as he tells it, of the world around him being changed . . . After leaping onto a fast-moving train carrying away the girl who had just rejected his marriage proposal, travelling without a ticket from Marburg to Berlin, sitting up all night and taking the

morning train back to Marburg still in a highly emotional condition, grieving, yet uplifted, twenty-one-year-old Pasternak
found, from that morning on, all his surroundings transformed:

I was surrounded by changed things. Something never before
experienced had crept into the essence of reality . . . Birds, houses,
dogs, trees, horses, tulips and people had all become shorter and
more abrupt than childhood had known them. The fresh laconicism
of life revealed itself to me, it crossed the road, took me by the hand
and led me along the pavement . . . Less than ever did I deserve
brotherhood with this vast summer sky. But, for the time being, all
was forgiven me.

Back in Marburg, unable to recognise the town, he aban-
doned philosophy, and began writing poetry. One of his early
poems, often regarded as seminal, is called 'Marburg'. It
starts:

> I shuddered, I flared like a flame and died out.
> I shook. I had just − made a proposal.
> Too late, it went wrong, the result − a refusal.
> How I pity her tears! I'm more bless'd than a saint.
>
> And out to the Square. You could say I was now
> like a person reborn. Every detail of things
> was alive and, completely neglectful of me,
> was arising in all of its sense of farewell.

Pasternak rarely theorised about literature. When he did, his
key concepts were the origination of the work of art in the life
of the artist and the experience of art as setting things in motion. All his work is full of examples of the first, and in *A
Safe Conduct* he writes:

What is experienced most immediately in the whole of art is precisely
its coming into being . . . We cease to recognise reality. It presents
itself in some new category. This category seems to us to be its, not
our, condition. Except for this condition, everything in the world
has been named. It alone is unnamed and new. We try to name it.
The result is art.

As everything is changed at once, any detail taken at random
will bear witness to the new condition (as, in the blowing canvas metaphor, every feature of the painting shows the same

movement). Accordingly his first poems were about 'the sea, the southern rain, the coal of the Harz' — just anything at all — and he had a feeling of 'solidarity' with the very 'gravel of the Giessen highway'.

And inspiration sets things in motion:

I always saw the goal in the changing of the depicted thing from cold axles to hot ones; in getting what had been outlived to set off in pursuit of life, to make it catch up with it.

'Life' rushes ahead, in this metaphor for artistic work of which Pasternak has offered many variants. Meanwhile most things lag behind, becoming 'turgid' and fixed: what art does is look back, with fear and pity, in order to excite those stopped things and set them in movement too. Both the response to change, and the passion for setting things going — if transferred to the national-historical scene — illumine Pasternak's welcoming of the Revolution.

He began writing prose as well as verse. His first prose attempts, found and published only a few years ago (some now available in translation in my *Pasternak on Art and Creativity*), show the same keen attention to the immediately surrounding urban, natural and domestic world and the same belief in the unimportance of the poet as a person. Not his inner life but the world — his outer life, as it were — is the subject: 'Every detail of things / was alive and, completely neglectful of me. . .' In *Doctor Zhivago* too there are many such originating moments of poetry, all stressing the aliveness of the world, and the subservience of the poet. Another connection with *Zhivago* is that the Marburg experience of inspiration through loss recurs in Yurii's burst of inspiration after losing Lara.

As a writer, the early Pasternak was concerned with earth and sky and vegetation, with domestic interiors and urban atmospheres, the world of 'things' altogether, with people if they were close to him or if he was in love with them (as he very often was) and with pondering the amazing genesis and transforming power of art. He was not concerned with history or politics or the social classes, with privilege and deprivation, nor with solving the horrendous problems of Russian society. Nor was he concerned with depicting everyday personal relations. He was sure he had something new to say. Nineteenth-century writers, it seemed to him, had fully worked out the description of personal and social behaviour, psychological analysis, study of moral and historical laws. Further, the 'civic' phase of literature in Russia in the later nineteenth century had fully explored the ways in which literature could unveil social ills and try to promote their disappearance, be a reformer, inciter, teacher. All this, he felt, was already done. Moreover, just as he began to write, the Symbolists had equally fully presented a view of literature as 'theurgic' – that is, as magically effective, creating or affirming links with a divine truth and leading to a transformation of the world through mystical forces. Pasternak had no inclination to repeat that either. His desire was to name what was 'as yet unnamed and new'. A certain existential strangeness had been offered to him, along with a gift to find expression for it which would be neither mystical nor matter-of-fact, neither naturalistic nor fantastic. Whatever he may have been doing in his non-writing life – taking part in political protest, grieving over the exploitation of women, rushing back to Moscow in 1917, working on Lenin in a Soviet archive, being a tutor, being a son, husband, father and friend – his life as a writer was focused on the task of finding language for his own peculiar novelty of vision. How valuable he felt this was, can be sensed in all he wrote about art in those years.

The last third of *A Safe Conduct* is dominated by the figure of Vladimir Mayakovsky, whom Pasternak met in 1914 and passionately admired. Though a poet, Mayakovsky came close to Pasternak's conception of the 'man of action'. He admired in him qualities he himself lacked: definiteness, decisiveness, the ability to project his personality into his appearance, his aura of destiny and doom and the way in which, unlike the lesser poets he collected around him, Mayakovsky played not 'roles' but 'life itself', adopting a 'pose' of total integrity. Mayakovsky is undoubtedly a prototype for Strelnikov, with his definiteness and talent for enacting his own life. In his poetry too, Mayakovsky was phenomenal, dazzling, and histrionic, and Pasternak, feeling his influence, wrenched himself free of it by renouncing in his own work what he called 'the Romantic manner', that is, all temptation to make a cult of the artist as a person. This was also the beginning of a long hard progress towards the 'heresy of an unheard-of simplicity'.

For Mayakovsky there was no question as to whether or not to accept the Revolution – 'it was my Revolution', he said. He flung himself into promoting it for more than a decade. Blok, after the October seizure of power, 'walked about young and merry and wide awake with shining eyes', seeing 'angels' wings behind the shoulders of every Red Guard soldier' (quoted from Avril Pyman's *Life of Aleksandr Blok*). He wrote his splendid paradoxical poem 'The Twelve', which differed from anything he had written before and was almost the last thing he was to write. Belyi, another outstanding Symbolist writer, left Russia but soon returned to stay, and responded to the Revolution with a long poem, 'Christ is Risen'. The peasant poet, Esenin, welcomed the Revolution too, as heralding Utopia for village life. Many writers shared the widespread feelings of liberation and immense hope, expectation of a new world without inequality or exploitation, with no more enormous wealth alongside desperate poverty: a new life for mankind, radiating from Russia. But others experienced the Revolution as disaster, the destruction of everything they valued, and went into exile; among the emigrants were the prose writer Ivan Bunin, the poet Zinaida Hippius, the writer and theorist Merezhkovsky.

Pasternak's response to events was both enthusiastic and watchful. Before discussing it, let us recall what were the main events preceding and during 1917. These constitute the historical subject-matter of most of *Doctor Zhivago*.

In the years after 1905, strikes and acts of violence against the government were resumed; then the war, which was felt to be a non-Russian war, led to still greater despair and anger. The fifteen million men called up were often poorly equipped, even without rifles; between five and eight million were killed.

The tsar's visit to the front in 1915 (described in *Doctor Zhivago*) left affairs of State in the hands of Rasputin, the debauched pseudo-monk (soon to be murdered by palace nobles) whose ascendance in the imperial household was clear proof of the demoralisation of the monarchy. There was starvation in the cities; thousands of workers went on strike. The first Revolution began on March 8th 1917 (February 23rd by the calendar then in use), when massive crowds gathered in the streets of Petersburg demanding food and an end to Russia's part in the war. Soldiers mutinied and joined the demonstrators, police stations were sacked and prisons unlocked. After six days, the tsar, 'Emperor of all the Russias', abdicated, and a liberal 'Provisional Government' was formed: four hundred years of autocracy had ended.

The year 1917, between the February and the October upheavals, was a time of unprecedented, and never repeated, freedoms. Censorship and secret police had vanished overnight, spontaneous meetings were held throughout the country, local 'soviets' (councils) were set up, ideas of all kinds were discussed as had never before been possible, and eccentric political experiments were undertaken. Blok wrote that spring:

Quite extraordinary is the feeling that nothing is forbidden — menacing, breathtaking and terribly exciting. Almost anything might happen and the moment . . . is a perilous one, but all is overcome by the awareness that a miracle has taken place and therefore we may expect more miracles . . . One thing is certain, and that is that a great deal more is going to happen, almost everybody feels this.

A great deal more did happen. After a series of crises, months of increasing hunger in both capitals, the Bolsheviks, who were the more revolutionary section of the Marxist and proletariat-oriented Social Democrats, headed by Vladimir Lenin, seized control of Petersburg in the course of twenty-four hours, on November 7th (October 25th) — with little difficulty or bloodshed. 'Soviet' power was proclaimed the following day. Meanwhile in Moscow there were ten days of fighting between Provisional Government supporters and Bolsheviks. The decrees which Yurii Zhivago reads in his newspaper as he shelters during that time from the blizzard would be Lenin's very first decrees ending Russia's commitment to the war, handing over the land to the peasants and control of production to the workers, and setting up a new government, the Council of People's Commissars.

Life in Russia became completely transformed. A whole way of life suddenly disappeared. The peasants kept the vast tracts of gentry-owned land they had seized; there was no more 'gentry'. Everything was nationalised – banks, railways, industries. The stock-market was abolished. There was no more large-scale private enterprise. Church property was confiscated, the enormous influence of the Church abruptly terminated. Courts of justice were replaced by 'revolutionary tribunals'; official ranks were done away with and all titles became Comrade. There were a myriad other reforms, including those of the calendar and the alphabet. Idealism ran feverishly high.

In a poem of 1919 Pasternak writes that

> In our days the very air smells of death.
> Opening a window is like opening veins –

a terrible sentiment from a poet to whom opened windows almost invariably meant life and inspiration. But the summer of 1917 had been experienced by him as a time of miracle. He was no anarchist, but he seems to have felt, as anarchists did, that the true Russian Revolution took place in those months, when people in their thousands were seizing possession of the land and taking factory after factory into their own hands.

When he heard of the February events, Pasternak came back to Moscow from his civilian war-work assignment in the Urals. During that year he wrote the poems of *My Sister Life*, the book that was to make his fame. Nearly all the poems are about love, nature, garden or forest, changes of weather, changes of mood, poetry itself; very few mention current events. Yet he felt the book to be directly about the national events and the atmosphere of that summer. When it finally came out, in 1922, Pasternak had a conversation (described by L. Fleishman) with the revolutionary leader Trotsky, who asked him why he 'abstained' from responding to social themes; he wished he had told Trotsky (not recording what he did tell him) that *My Sister Life* was

revolutionary in the best sense of the word. That the phase of revolution closest to the heart and to poetry — the *morning* of revolution, its outburst, when it returns man to the *nature* of man and looks at the State with the eyes of *natural* right . . . are expressed by this book in its very spirit.

I will quote the poem that bears the volume's title — better translated, if the metre allowed it, as 'Life is my Sister':

> My sister is life and today in a teeming
> it's crashed on us all like a flood of spring rain,
> yet wearers of watch-chains are snobbish and peevish
> and sting you politely like snakes in the grain.
>
> Our elders have reasons for this. Whereas yours
> is of course, of course, a preposterous reason
> for eyes and lawns turning lilac in storms
> and horizons smelling of damp reséda,
>
> and for railway timetables, read in May,
> on your journey, down a provincial line,
> being more majestic than Holy Scripture
> or couches blackened by wind and grime.
>
> And when brakes break out in a bark and collide
> with the villagers tippling peacefully,
> there's gazing from mattresses: this my stop?
> and the sun as it sets is condolent with me.
>
> And the bell floats off at its third-time splash
> in a flowing apology: sorry, not here.
> A smell of singed night wafts under the blind
> and the land falls away between footboard and star.
>
> Winking, blinking, but somewhere they're sleeping,
> and like a mirage my beloved sleeps
> while my heart goes splashing along the compartments
> and scatters the carriage-doors in the steppes.

The exultant elaborate orchestration of vowels and consonants that makes this poem ring with energy cannot be carried across in English. However we can see that, although the slap at the dressed-up people accords with current anti-bourgeois feeling, the pleasure in how storms affect the colour of grass or how the horizon smells in the rain is less than obviously socio-political, as is the traveller's delight in trains, rural glimpses and the thought of people asleep. Nonetheless, from the crashing flood of life in the first lines to the final plunging of the land and rebellious water-like action of the heart, the poem is full of a gladness, excitement and impatience which could well be understood as a private response to national eventfulness.

When Marina Tsvetaeva read *My Sister Life*, she felt utterly overwhelmed and recognised Pasternak's talent as kindred to her own. She spread her arms out wide 'so that the joints all cracked' and said she 'was caught in it as in a downpour'. And she wrote − a judgment that proved very apt: 'Pasternak's word about the Revolution, like the Revolution's word about itself, is still to come. In the summer of 1917 he walked in step with it, carefully listening.'

Chapter 3

Pasternak's life, work and times after 1917

Unlike Zhivago, Pasternak stayed in Moscow during the Civil War — years of great hardship for everyone, with hunger, typhoid and unbearable cold. Like very many others, he and his brother broke up the rafters from their roof and all but the most essential furniture, to use as fuel.

When Emma Goldman, the anarchist writer banished under tsarism, returned in 1920, she found Petersburg 'almost in ruins, as if a hurricane had swept over it', but in Moscow, despite the ubiquitous Cheka (the new secret police), life was 'intense, varied and interesting', with unprecedented street markets where proletarian and aristocrat, Communist and bourgeois, stood side by side, to sell and buy: 'Here one could find for sale a rusty iron pot alongside of an exquisite icon.' Her description is very similar to that in *Doctor Zhivago*, as is her account of chaos on the railways: travellers waiting for weeks on the platforms; steps and roofs of carriages so crowded that soldiers resorted to arms to get people off, 'scores of passengers swept to their death by low bridges'.

Meanwhile the vast countryside of Russia was torn by fighting between the Reds, or Bolsheviks (aided by numerous partisan units like the one which kidnaps Zhivago), and the Whites — Mensheviks, liberal democrats, monarchists and many others. The aspect of the war described in the novel is that in the east, where, in the Siberian town of Omsk, in March 1919, Admiral Kolchak had set up a rival government, with himself as 'Supreme Ruler'. Kolchak is the only historical figure given any prominence in the novel. After some victories, his armies were forced back, and he was driven out of Omsk later that year, to be captured in January 1920 and executed in February.

By giving Yurii nearly two years with the partisans, starting in spring 1919, yet having him leave them just after the capture of Kolchak, Pasternak expands one year into two — perhaps to discourage an interest in mere chronology, perhaps by mistake, or possibly for another reason. There are several instances of confused dating in *Doctor Zhivago*, generally in relation to historical events or social conditions, and in more than one case a deliberate and overt vagueness is linked with a change in narratorial point of view. An example is the paragraph about the three Civil War winters as experienced in Moscow:

There were three of them in a row, those terrible winters, one after another, and not everything that seems now to have happened between 1917 and 1918 really did happen then, but happened, perhaps, later. Those winters, one following the other, merged together, and it is difficult to separate one from another.　　　　　(6:9)

Questions are begged here: to whom does it 'seem' that some things happened later? And — what things? 'Merged' in whose mind? It cannot be Yurii's, given the present tense and the word 'now', and Pasternak has not created any fictional narrator with a memory and a present of his own. So it has to be in Pasternak's own mind that these winters are confounded. As in several other places, he enters his text as biographical author, as though parts of it were his memoir. The awkward tone of the quoted paragraph, with its 'perhaps' and its excessive repetition of 'one after another', seems to betray an unclear desire to combine his own experience (of the three Moscow winters) with his hero's (of the first one only) as well as a certain simple-heartedness, as if he were saying: An imperfection? Well, so be it, I can't do it any other way. Or as if a sculptor were displaying a partly shaped statue along with the rough stone from which it is being carved.

Whatever its vagueness about dates, the novel gives an accurate enough picture of the horrors of the time. Along the main highways and in other places where fighting was going on, villages and towns endured a repeated alternation of government, as first one side, then the other, conquered the district, each change bringing arrests, executions and

murders. There was hunger in the countryside too, with
agricultural production only half what it had been in 1914.
Armed squads sent out to requisition grain did not flinch
from killing peasants who refused to hand it over. Bandits
and robbers flourished, orphaned children roamed the roads,
and, as Pasternak writes, 'Those days justified the ancient
saying that "man is a wolf to man".'

After the final Bolshevik victory, Lenin suspended the
policies of War Communism and, to save the damaged
economy, brought in his temporary 'New Economic Policy':
grain seizure was stopped and free enterprise on a small scale
was re-introduced. Back came the old commercialism with all
its trappings, and to many the NEP seemed a betrayal of the
Revolution's ideals; in *Doctor Zhivago* it is called 'the most
false and ambiguous of Soviet periods'.

More than two-thirds of the text of *Zhivago* is devoted to
the years of Revolution and Civil War. Pasternak was writing
about it all thirty to forty years after the event. But during the
1920s, Revolution and Civil War were the most popular
subject-matter of novels and stories. Babel's finely wrought
miniatures, for example, and Pilnyak's stylistically inventive
Bare Year, dealt with these subjects, as did more traditional
novels such as Fadeev's pseudo-Tolstoyan *Rout* and Sholo-
khov's *Quiet Don*.

The twenties were a uniquely interesting time in Russian
literature. Having to think out the relation of literature to a
transformed society and to a new public ideology, writers
formed innumerable groups, each with its theory, attitude
and style. For a while Pasternak belonged uneasily to 'Lef',
a group led by Mayakovsky, which was fervently Marxist and
tendentious. Other prominent groups were the short-lived
Proletkult, which sought to create a specifically proletarian
culture; Pereval (The Divide), revolutionary too, but
humanistic and more respectful of tradition; and the Sera-
pions, who shared with one another solely their refusal
to share any theory. How to convey the experience of violence and upheaval was one general preoccupation. How to

respond, personally, as a writer, to the new order of things was another. But the heady time of debate and experiment began sobering off in the mid-twenties, as the formidable Russian Association of Proletarian Writers, known as RAPP, gained influence. RAPP, which held that 'all ideological doubts are absolutely inadmissible', heralded the outlawing of talent and the instituting of dullness that was to be Soviet literature's lot in the thirties.

Just as the Civil War would not become Pasternak's theme for another twenty years, so his relation to the new regime was, as Tsvetaeva had foreseen, clarified only very slowly and thoughtfully. He was uplifted by the aspirations embodied in the Revolution and continued to feel that he was one of those who, in the words of the poet Tyutchev, are 'blessed to have visited this world in its moment of fate'. Not wishing to lose touch with what was happening in the country at large, he decided on a change of poetic genre. 'I consider that epic is prompted by the age', he said in 1927, 'and therefore in my book *The Year 1905* I am moving from lyric thinking to epic, though it is very difficult.' Both that work and *Lieutenant Schmidt* go back to 1905 for their subject-matter, while two other epic-length poems deal with 1917 and its aftermath – 'Lofty Malady' (containing a strong stanza in praise of the rapier-like decisiveness of Lenin) and the novel in verse, 'Spektorsky'. But the style of all four works is dense and difficult ('1905' somewhat less so), not at all the accessible style required by 'the age'.

None of his epic works seemed to Pasternak successful; something in them went against the grain for him, and often he felt he had a different 'word' to say about Russia in and after revolution. Shortly after the letter just quoted, he told his cousin Olga Freidenberg of another duty: to write of

the decade just past, its events, its meaning and so on, only not in the objective-epical way as I did in 'The Year 1905', but in a personal, subjective depiction – i.e. I shall have to tell of how we all saw and experienced it. I shall not move a step forward either in life or in work if I don't report to myself on this piece of time. I have to write about this.

This 'report' would include the more sinister truths, for the letter goes on to mention the current renewal of State 'terror'. Thus two different impulses of conscience moved Pasternak to change his subject matter and genre, the one relating to the age's grandeur, the other to its horror. Both lead towards *Doctor Zhivago*.

Another motive for change was that his work was so often misunderstood, being regarded as esoteric and 'remote from the epoch'. Lunacharsky, first Commissar for Education, called Pasternak 'foggy, strange, unintelligible in the extreme, unsuited to our epoch'. Critics repeated endlessly that, while 'brilliant', he was essentially an 'indoors' (*komnatnyi*) poet, or a 'chamber' (*kamernyi*) poet, using an analogy with chamber-music – refined music for few instruments, played in a house to a selected audience; and in 1934 the influential Bukharin actually defended him by saying he was 'enclosed in the mother-of-pearl shell of individual experiences, very tender and fine, the fragile quiverings of a wounded, easily woundable, soul'. Yet there was never anything fragile or indoorish about Pasternak's work, and these parrot-like descriptions of it were due partly to its relative difficulty and partly to the fact that it was not made up of clichés and familiar generalisations about the heroic Soviet age. Pasternak was not closed in at all, but was very much an outdoors, real-world poet, robust and not vulnerable, wholly attuned to atmospheres and truths outside himself. 'Not I but the world', one critic has summed up his general stance. Moreover, for Pasternak, art always arose in response to a challenge, or 'cry', or 'imperative' coming to him from the outside world.

Response to challenge is a motif in most of Pasternak's earlier fiction, of which I want to make a brief survey here, to see how it points forward to *Doctor Zhivago*. For in the novel he expresses, again and again, in new and simpler form, the feelings, ideas and questions which had preoccupied him in his ealier prose writing.

In the first story Pasternak published, 'The Mark of

Apelles', written in 1915, one poet challenges another to speak of love in a single perfect line. The second poet, who believes that 'all our lives we are upon a stage', challenges the idea of a merely technical perfection by taking the matter over into real life and — with perfect artistry and staging — seducing the first poet's mistress. The story is a tour-de-force, and is about a tour-de-force, an aesthetic duel fought out in the frontierless world of art, for the second poet is mysteriously named 'Heine' and the setting is the beautiful Italian city of Ferrara. In subsequent stories, the protagonist looks increasingly outward, into society and history.

'The Childhood of Lyuvers', written in 1918, is generally regarded as Pasternak's prose masterpiece. It is one of the only two of his fictional works that do not have a poet as central character, though it too contains a sort of challenge — that which confronts its younger heroine (a forerunner of Lara) in the disturbing significance she senses in a stranger, 'the other person'. Through responding to this, and through the vividly depicted details of the world around her, she learns and grows. Tangibly set in Russia, as all the subsequent stories are, this is a moral and personal study, of how external things, whether marvellous, uncanny or commonplace, are internalised by a sensitive child; how a conscious personality comes into being.

A new dimension enters Pasternak's prose with the story 'Letters from Tula' (1918). This too is about art and morality, but what is new in it is an explicit awareness of the twentieth century, and of the challenge presented by modernity. It is a study of the shame felt by someone becoming aware of art's potentiality for falsehood. Each half of the story focuses on a different lonely artist. In the first, a poet sits in a waiting-room at Tula station before his return to Moscow, writing letters to a woman-friend he has seen off on a long journey. He tells her of his dismay when a film actor, one of a troupe making a historical film in the meadows nearby, comes up and addresses him as 'colleague'. Sickened by the actors' lack of seriousness and histrionic behaviour even when off the set, he nonetheless recognises himself in them, but feels 'there is no place left in the world where a person could warm his soul with the fire of shame; everywhere shame has got damp and won't burn'. Tula, bound up with the life of Tolstoy, is the very 'territory of conscience', and shame does seem to burn the poet, but he gets no further than formulating his need for 'a complete physical silence' and his belief that 'everything would begin when he ceased hearing himself'. However, in the second half of the story, what the poet sought in vain is attained by an aged ex-actor, unconnected with him, who has also been dismayed by the film actors and, alone in his room, acts out a role from the past so well that he weeps and seems transfigured.

Here the theme of acting has polarised into false public posturing and true solitary drama, a polarity which will be basic to *Doctor Zhivago* with its interest in two kinds of mimicry (see chapter 5, pp. 79f. below), and with all its expressions of distrust for oratory and of longing for a fundamental quiet: 'How one longs sometimes to get away from all the untalentedly exalted, cheerless, human word-mongering and go off into the seeming silence of nature.' (5:5)

The one early piece that comes close to dealing with contemporary events is 'Aerial Ways'. 'Without actually entering the hemisphere of historical concerns', writes Christopher Barnes, 'Pasternak is now skirting its extremities and charting those aerial ways of history that only men like Lenin and Liebknecht can safely tread'. In this story, a woman twice loses her son: first when gipsies carry the baby off into the fields and secondly when, years later, the youth is sentenced to execution during the Revolution. As in *Doctor Zhivago*, mixed praise and lament are implied for the unswerving 'aerial' thoughts of the revolutionary activists, which contrast with the muddle and hopelessness of folk who get lost in the fields of history and lose their children there. This 'challenge' is one that cannot be met: personal life cannot duel with the forces of history.

Pasternak's last lengthy fictional work before *Doctor Zhivago* is the unfinished story 'A Tale'. Here, the motif of acting has become entwined with that of total response to an external need. Seryozha, a poet on leave from war service, reflects how he once began writing a tale, wanting to distribute the money it would earn amongst distressed women, hoping the event, starting locally, like 'what happened in Galilee', would spread world-wide and 'renew the universe'. His tale concerns a man who (like the old actor in 'Letters from Tula') achieves the poet's own aim — by offering himself, body and soul, for sale at an auction, with the proviso that he should have the time to distribute the money among women. Recommending himself to bidders, he performs on stage, brilliantly, as musician and poet-reciter. But what is now seen as the essence of art is not perfection of performance, as it was in 'The Mark of Apelles', or the silence of honesty, as in 'Letters from Tula'; instead it is martyrdom, a sheer act for others — the man is ready to be tortured or killed by his buyer. Only total self-giving can make art the deed of rescue which Pasternak believed it must be. Seryozha's reflections abruptly end when Lemokh, a 'dry, definite and very rapid man', arrives and he finds himself 'confronting something tall and alien that devalued him from head to foot. It was the masculine spirit of fact, that most modest and terrible of spirits.' In chapter 5 I shall discuss the connection between this sharply outlined yet enigmatic figure who silently negates the poet's whole being and the similar but less effective Strelnikov, in the novel.

Closest of all to the novel is the autobiographical work *A Safe Conduct*. Some of its sentences reappear in *Doctor Zhivago* in 'smoothed out and unnoticeable' form, and many of its themes are expanded there; indeed in 1946 Pasternak called his novel 'the world of *A Safe Conduct* once again, only without the theorising'. Almost everything in *A Safe Conduct* is related to the theme of the origination of art in an individual, 'biographical' life. Scent of narcissi in a Moscow cellar, the uneven gait of a German professor over cobbles, gondolas sliding between Venetian palaces: all the evoked sensations somehow lead to art, or spring from the randomness art delights in, or recall the unique freshness of creativity. In *Doctor Zhivago*, too, the story tends constantly

towards evocations or accounts of poetic creation. Further,
Part 1 of *A Safe Conduct* is much concerned with the question why most people forfeit, as Pasternak sees it, their
chance of uniqueness, originality, and instead choose to be
conventional, fixed and conformist. As in *Zhivago*, it is taken
for granted that dullness is not innate, but that people
choose it for some unknown reason. 'Why have the majority
departed in the shape of an acceptable commonness?'
'Tradition' itself offers each one a unique face or personhood
(in Russian the word for 'face', *litso*, is also one of the words
for 'personality'), yet most are content with the 'tedious
cooking' of life's ingredients, not realising that life begins
when you 'dine off the finished dish'. This concern prefigures
Zhivago's lament that the revolutionaries, after their moment
of action, do not know how to live but can only prepare to
do so. A third important theme common to the two works is
the contrast between the active person who lives by self-
projection and the more receptive or passive person who lives
in a kind of self-effacement. Strelnikov and Zhivago are pre-
enacted by Mayakovsky and Pasternak as depicted in *A Safe
Conduct*.

The six prose works I have surveyed are copiously
metaphorical yet carefully chiselled compositions which
repeatedly astonish the reader with image, syntax and idea.
Pasternak never wrote such prose again. In subsequent years
he was motivated by what he felt to be a moral and historical
imperative: 'to have a *direct* conversation with the age "about
life and death", the conversation Stalin had refused him in
1934' (I am quoting E. B. Pasternak and V. M. Borisov in
Novyi mir, June 1988). 'Direct' meant simple, accessible, unpretentious, aiming not for perfect artistry but for universal
significance. One letter describes these hopes in a telling series
of epithets: he would write something 'worthwhile, human, in
prose, greyly, boringly and modestly, something large and
nourishing'. The prose attempts of those years were steps
towards the novel: fragments published in the late 1930s have
a first-person narrator in whose name, 'Zhivult', the syllable
'zhiv' means 'alive' as it does in 'Zhivago' (an earlier hero

was called 'Purvit', made up from the French words 'pour
vie'); Zhivult's thoughts prefigure Zhivago's and he tells
a story which starts in 1905 and was to move on into the
twenties, as the novel would do.

1929, the year Zhivago dies, was the year in which Stalin
ended the NEP and began to implement his first Five Year
Plan for economic development. It was also the year in which
Russian literature started finding itself under serious threat.
Articles in *Pravda* called for a 'consolidation of literary
forces', and instructed writers to celebrate the Plan and write
about industrial construction enterprises. Four years before
this, an ominous step had been taken by the Communist
Party when it issued a decree promising tolerance towards
'fellow-travellers' (meaning non-Communist writers who did
not actually oppose Communism), for it thereby implied that
it had the right and the power to exercise and withdraw such
tolerance. The same decree stated that 'the style consonant
with the epoch' would soon be found − to oust other styles.
In his idiosyncratic response to the decree, Pasternak wrote:
'I felt the breath of history which the Resolution *wished to*
breathe' (my italics). The power of RAPP became stifling in
the late 1920s, then in 1932 all groups and associations were
summarily disbanded by Party decree and writers were
recombined in one institution, the Soviet Writers' Union,
which soon became the powerful body it still is today, following dictates from above and keeping literature under political
control. For various reasons, including relief at being out of
the clutches of RAPP, many joined in what has been called
the 'cult of enthusiastic unanimity' in the early thirties, and
at the Union's first Congress 'socialist realism' was proclaimed the one suitable style.

  Clearly, a writer may not find it natural or honest to write
about current events, or may need to write about them in an
indirect fashion, or may need years of thinking and feeling to
allow them to find their relation to the inner space he or she
inhabits before they can become the 'subject' of a poem or
novel. The disaster which overtook Russian literature in the

middle decades of this century resulted from the philistine assumption that good writing may come not from such thinking and feeling but from obedience to command; or rather, from the combination of that assumption with governmental force. There was inspiration and vision in the making of the Revolution, but there was none in the subsequent official attitude to the arts. The conviction that all things could be planned and everyone without exception included in the plan, and the fanatic readiness to call one style virtuous and other styles (labelled 'formalism' or 'naturalism', for example) criminal, led to a persecution of originality infinitely more destructive than what happened in the repressive tsarist times.

At the 1934 Congress Pasternak sat on the platform with other members of the new Writers' Union, full of good will and hoping to hear words of inspiration. At one point he provoked laughter by appearing eccentrically out of touch with the times: on to the platform had marched a delegation of building workers led by a woman bearing aloft some heavy tool to symbolise the dignity of work – whereupon he had leapt to his feet and offered to carry it for her. Not just the old-world chivalry, but the sheer personal quality, of such behaviour conflicted with the generalities and tub-thumping about the glory of Soviet literature and disintegration of other cultures that filled the main speeches at the Congress. Pasternak grew less hopeful as the days passed and he complained to a friend in one of the intervals that the falsity of manner and the low level of thought was making him 'murderously depressed'.

When it came to his own, very short, speech on the thirteenth day, he made no reference to previous discussion, even though much of it had been about him – the question was arising as to whether he should be promoted to 'first' Soviet poet (if so, he would have to overcome his 'indoors' quality and take on the material of the Revolution). He told the audience that what was far more valuable than official speeches was the silent exchange of feeling between people at the Congress and the poetry born spontaneously in that process; poetry, he went on to say, was 'prose, the voice of prose, the language of organic fact'.

These paradoxes were outdone by the enigmatic oxymoron he offered his audience the following year when, now chronically depressed but forced to go to Paris to the Congress of Writers in Defence of Culture, he said (in a still shorter speech) that poetry was 'a height, higher than any alps, which lies in the grass underfoot'; moreover, it was too simple to be discussed at conferences. Seven months later he spoke yet again at a literary conference in Minsk.

This time he had something more disturbing to say, bitterly criticising fellow-writers and announcing a radical change in himself. He lamented the 'elevated trumpeting vulgarity' that had become established in talk about literature (the words are almost exactly reproduced in *Doctor Zhivago*), the habit of indulgence in 'literary banqueting', the 'depravity of stage readings' which made poetry a 'fairground entertainment', and the wide acceptance of ideas hostile to creativity, such as that the harder you work the more poems you'll produce, like working a pump handle. By conforming to official requirements and by canonising ideological rhetoric, writers were losing touch with art itself, for 'art is unthinkable without risk and spiritual self-sacrifice'. He went on to say that in his own creative work he intended to move on to new themes, a transition that would have to be accomplished 'in a space that had become rarefied by journalistic abstractions'. In case it sounded like a promise to start conforming, he added: 'on these themes that are common to us all I shall not speak in the common tongue, I shall not repeat you, comrades, but shall argue with you'. The new mode would be difficult for him and, with his 'grey, boring and modest' expectations in mind, he confessed: 'for a while I shall write like a cobbler, forgive me'. That it required courage to state that writing poetry was not like pumping water from a well, and even more, to say, as he did on a still more dangerous occasion a month later, that telling a poet to adopt one topic rather than another was as ludicrous as telling a woman to give birth to a girl, not a boy, shows how powerful the destructive attitude to art had become. After this, the idea of making Pasternak the 'first poet' was dropped.

Between the Minsk congress and Pasternak's starting regular work on *Doctor Zhivago* lay ten years of terrible national suffering: Stalin's euphemistically named 'purges' and the Second World War. The amount of suffering there has been in Russia in our century cannot be imagined. From the First World War to the second, successive waves of destruction brought unnatural deaths that have to be counted in millions. In the collectivisation of agriculture − 'liquidating' the richer peasants and compelling the poorer into collective farms − and in the famine resulting from it, it is said that almost four million people lost their lives. Now, perhaps twelve million died, in the worst of the purge years. Many had died in earlier purges. The fact that twenty million Russians were killed in the Second World War has always been much publicised; yet before it the same number may have perished at Stalin's hands.

Terror was practised by the Bolshevik state from its inception, but in 1936–38 it reached unprecedented dimensions. Arbitrary arrests on a massive scale, fake trials, banishments, imprisonments, tortures, executions − these became everyday occurrences. In a monstrous chain of mutual denunciations, with one day's jailer becoming next day's jailed (the head of the secret police, Yezhov, himself became a victim), two-thirds of the governing classes destroyed themselves; many faithful Communists were tried and shot. Among the millions who disappeared, it has been calculated there were some 600 known writers. Among some of the more famous of these: Babel was arrested and murdered; Pilnyak died in prison; the poet Zabolotsky was sent to a camp for years; the poet Klyuyev also died in a prison camp; Mandelstam, who has been called the greatest poet of our time, was deported to his death in a far eastern camp; two Georgian poets, who were Pasternak's close friends, died − Yashvili committing suicide on hearing of the arrest and torture of Tabidze. Another close friend of Pasternak's, Tsvetaeva, who had left Russia in 1922, came back in 1939, full of mistaken hope, and hanged herself two years later. The whole of Soviet society was damaged by the atmosphere of threat, fear, and suspicion in those years. Nadezhda Mandelstam, widow of the poet, describes in her memoirs what it felt like to 'live among people who vanished into exile, labour camps or the other world and also among those who sent them there', to live with the feeling that 'we were constantly exposed to x-rays'. After 1937, she says, 'people stopped meeting each other altogether'.

Despite verbal attacks, Pasternak was never arrested. When he entitled his autobiography *A Safe Conduct*, he seems to have foreseen his survival of the terror to come. But how did he survive? By good luck? By the inscrutability of his style (which made it hard to attach an accusation of wrong opinion to his writings)? Through a whim of Stalin's? Or because of his translations from the Georgian (Stalin was Georgian)? Or, thanks to influential benefactors? The mysterious protector figure in the novel, Evgraf, may be a product of his awareness of having been somehow protected from on high. In fact there is a whole series of protectors in *Doctor Zhivago*, testifying to the near-impossibility of living without them. Samdevyatov derives his name from San Donato, suggesting gifts, and may represent the provision of material goods, while Evgraf, whose name is Greek for 'good writing', probably represents survival as a creator; he enables Yurii to write in difficult conditions, and he saves and sorts the poet's posthumous manuscripts.

Yet Zhivago dies before the thirties. Some commentators think Pasternak was transferring the thirties' atmosphere back into the twenties. Others point out that the twenties were already years of terror and of the need for protection. In either case, it is clear that Pasternak was not ready to write about the purges. Reluctance to make historical violence his theme is already noticeable in *A Safe Conduct*. It tells its story up to 1914, then, with the remarkable understatement 'Six years passed', moves ahead briefly to 1920, then quickly on to 1930 to mourn the death of a friend. The chronology is repeated in Pasternak's second autobiography, which was written in the 1950s and so omits the later period of violence as well − and it too jumps briefly ahead, to 1941, to mourn the death of friends. In *Zhivago* Pasternak finally does take the Civil War period as his subject. But by ending the main narrative in 1929 — with the Epilogue jumping briefly ahead, first to 1943 and then to 'five or ten years later' (ten would make it the year of Stalin's death) — he palpably avoids dwelling on that destructive period.

Two years after Pasternak's death, another Russian writer to become famous in the west and to be awarded the Nobel Prize, Alexander Solzhenitsyn, impressively entered the literary scene with his *One Day in the Life of Ivan Denisovich*, the first published description of one of Stalin's concentration camps. Solzhenitsyn has taken up with energy the task Pasternak had not felt was his: to lay bare all the suffering, expose the crimes, accuse the criminals, uncover origins and motives. The essential truth about our age, according to Solzhenitsyn, 'though not entirely made up of prisons, executions, camps and places of exile', nonetheless 'cannot be told in full if you overlook them'. Pasternak does not overlook them, but he works at a far different pace and with different passions. His care not to overlook them is seen in the way he insistently alludes to them, though in brusque and cursory statements, such as the tacked-on remark at the end of Part 15 of *Doctor Zhivago* that Lara was 'apparently arrested in those days on the street and died or vanished somewhere unknown, forgotten under some nameless number . . . in one of the innumerable general or women's camps of the north'. Another example is the retrospective opinion of Misha Gordon that 'collectivisation was a false and unsuccessful measure, and the mistake could not be admitted. To hide the failure, every means of deterrence had to be used to stop people judging and thinking and to force them to see what was not there . . . Hence the unparalleled cruelty of the Yezhov terror.' (16:2)

In a postscript to his *Autobiographical Sketch*, Pasternak writes:

To continue *Doctor Zhivago* further would have been beyond my powers . . . One would have to speak . . . of a world of earlier unknown aims and aspirations, tasks and exploits, of a new restraint, new severity and new ordeals . . . One would have to write of it in such a way that the heart would falter and the hair would stand on end. To write of it automatically and ordinarily, to write of it other than overwhelmingly, to write more pallidly than Gogol and Dostoevsky depicted Petersburg, is not only senseless and aimless but base and shameful. We are still far from this ideal.

The abstractness of this passage shows it was meant to be published in the Soviet Union. But Pasternak is clearly saying that, censorship or not, he himself could not do such writing. What he could do was something very different.

'For the first time in my life I want to write something really genuine', Pasternak wrote to his cousin in December 1945, and added: 'I've suddenly become terribly free.' Nine months later he told her: 'One cannot put off forever the free expression of one's real thoughts. What I have done this year amounts to the first steps on this path and they are extraordinary.' Later that year he wrote: 'This is my first real work. In it I want to give a historical picture of Russia in the last forty years . . . This work will be the expression of my views on art, on the Gospels, on human life in history and much else. The atmosphere of the work is my Christianity.' The approach he was taking was unfamiliar to him and he wrote, to another friend: 'I am writing too disconnectedly, not the way a writer writes'; but he never felt estranged from it, and he said, over the next few years: 'This is the first work I have ever been proud of in my life'; 'My ultimate happiness and madness is the novel in prose'; 'Joyfully and unhesitatingly I am giving myself up to forces which are simplifying my thought and language, deepening my fate and rapidly broadening my tasks.'

In 1948, again to his cousin Olga, Pasternak wrote of his feeling of indebtedness: 'There are people who love me very much — my heart is in debt to them. For them I am writing this novel, writing it as my big long letter to them'; and, 'I am guilty towards everyone. But what am I to do? So the novel is part of this debt of mine, a proof that I did at least try.'

The certainty that, in writing it, he was himself changing

was very strong in Pasternak, along with his uncertainty about the book's own future. 'I am writing a novel', he wrote to a friend in 1952, 'and see it in my mind as a published book; but just when it will be published, in 10 months or in 50 years, I neither know nor care . . . Please don't consider me an important poet. For one thing, I've never been that, and for another, you will see what I am really going to be.' The following year, he wrote to someone else: 'with complete lightheartedness, I sit down to my Zhivago, which no one needs and which is inseparable from me', and, over the next two years, while writing the final sections of the novel, he wrote (to several correspondents): 'I have finished the rough draft of the narrative of the content of a novel and hope to finish it by the spring. You'll hear of me in quite a different way, you'll see me in a wholly new light', 'from every side I hear: why are you writing prose? is that your business?', 'This is a labour for the soul, a labour which will never see the light of day or only in the distant future.'

Doubts about the success of the new style were expressed in letters to several correspondents: 'The desire which pursues me more and more, to write modestly without special effects or stylistic coquetries, has probably taken me too far.' 'I am copying out the second book of my novel, making alterations at almost every stage. I began writing it in those post-war years when I lost artistic concentration, inwardly declined, like a weakened violin string or bowstring − I wrote this prose *unprofessionally*, without a consciously sustained artistic aim, domestically − in the bad sense, with a kind of greyness and naivety which I allowed and forgave myself. It's uneven, not many will like it. But I could do no otherwise.' Both these quotations are from 1955, in which year, however, he also wrote to a friend: 'You can't imagine how much is achieved! Names have been found for all that witchcraft that has tormented, bewildered and depressed us for so many decades. Everything has been sorted out and named, simply, transparently, sadly. And once again fresh, new definitions have been given to all that's most loved and important.'

By 1956 the novel was practically completed, and Pasternak

put these words into the postscript of his *Autobiographical Sketch*: 'I am finishing my chief and most important work, the only one of which I am not ashamed and for which I boldly answer – a novel in prose with a supplement of poems, *Doctor Zhivago*. The poems scattered throughout all the years of my life and those collected in this book are preparatory steps towards the novel.' His judgment on his own earlier work was repeated in many letters, as in one he wrote in English to Thomas Merton, after the book's publication, saying: 'Except the Doctor Zhivago all the rest of my verses and writings are devoid of any sense and importance.'

Synopsis of the events narrated in the novel

The novel opens in 1902 with the funeral of Yurii Zhivago's mother and the suicide of his father. Yurii is ten and staying with his uncle. In Part 2, while workers' strikes and street demonstrations are taking place in 1905, Lara, a schoolgirl, is seduced by a rich lawyer, Komarovsky, and Yurii – being brought up in the professorial family of Alexander and Anna Gromeko – catches a glimpse of her in her mother's dingy hotel after an elegant musical evening at the Gromekos' has been interrupted.

Part 3 shows Yurii and Lara growing up in their different spheres; their paths cross again at another interrupted party when Lara fires a gun and Yurii is called away by news of Anna Gromeko's death; this is in 1911. The two become acquainted four years later (Part 4). Both have married: Yurii marries the Gromekos' daughter Tonya (Antonina) and Lara marries Pasha (Pavel) Antipov, son of a railway worker. Both find themselves at the front during the First World War – Yurii as doctor, Lara as a nurse searching for her vanished husband. Their meeting coincides with news of the February Revolution. Part 5 describes incidents resulting from the Revolution that take place in a small provincial town called Melyuzeev where Yurii and Lara are working; in the atmosphere of the Revolution, he falls in love with her.

Lara is absent from Parts 6, 7 and 8, as well as from 10, 11 and 12, but in Parts 7 and 8 Yurii travels, unawares, towards a new meeting with her. In Part 6, having returned to Moscow, he throws a last party, the talkative spirit of which is again interrupted — by a thunderstorm; then during the hard year of 1917 he treats patients, cares for his family, and adapts himself to the conditions that follow the Bolshevik coup in October, soon assisted by his *deus ex machina* half-brother Evgraf, who advises the family to go to Tonya's former family estate, Varykino, far off in Siberia. They leave by train in April 1918 and travel for weeks, talking to diverse fellow passengers, and finally reaching the Siberian town Yuryatin. Part 7 ends with a strange and important meeting, the first of two that Yurii has with the revolutionary activist Strelnikov (Lara's husband, formerly known as Pasha Antipov).

In Part 8, which opens Volume II, the family travel on, meet one Samdevyatov who later helps them, and arrive at Varykino where they settle in a broken-down annexe to the house and work hard at making a living from the land. Much of Part 9 consists of the diary Yurii keeps during the year or so they spend there. A chance reunion with Lara in Yuryatin (the town where she once lived with her husband) leads to the beginning of their love affair, interrupted when Yurii is kidnapped by Bolshevik partisan fighters in need of a doctor. It is now summer 1919; he is taken to the heart of the Civil War raging in the countryside.

Through the thoughts of Galuzina, a character who appears solely in Part 10 (from which the novel's main characters are absent), effects of Revolution and Civil War are shown in another Siberian town; here, too, a clandestine Bolshevik meeting is held, and a celebratory party for recruits to the White Army is violently interrupted. Attention returns to Yurii in Parts 11 and 12. Sharing the partisans' movements and encampments, he works as a doctor, requisitions medicines, is present at a battle, talks with their leader, Liverii, overhears a conspiracy and witnesses atrocities; after a year and a half he makes his escape.

In Yuryatin, which has been held by the Whites but is now

finally Red, Yurii lives with Lara, working in his profession, for most of a year — which must be 1920 as it follows the defeat of Kolchak. But in Part 14 Komarovsky (not heard of since Part 2) turns up out of the blue to warn them of the danger they are in from the new authorities: just as he once left Moscow for Varykino with his wife and child (who have now emigrated), Yurii now leaves Yuryatin for Varykino with Lara and her child. This time the idyll there of peace and creative work only lasts two weeks; Komarovsky saves Lara from wolves and Bolsheviks by taking her away to the far east. Left alone, Yurii has his second strange meeting with Strelnikov, who turns up unexpectedly and talks for hours before carrying out his plan to kill himself.

Part 15 covers the next eight years. Yurii gets back to Moscow, on foot, in spring 1922, there to make a poor living and publish some of his writings, setting up house with Marina, the daughter of his former servant. Just after starting on a new creative period, he dies of a heart attack. Lara turns up to find his body lying in the very room occupied long ago by her husband-to-be. The year is 1929.

Part 16 leaps to 1943, the middle of the Second World War. Yurii's two friends, Gordon and Dudorov, talk of their army and prison experiences, and Tanya, a young linen-keeper who tells of childhood miseries and horrors, turns out to be the lost daughter of Yurii and Lara; she will be protected by the powerful Evgraf Zhivago. 'Five or ten years later', in Moscow, the same two friends read Yurii's books and meditate on the future of Russia.

Chapter 4

The opening of *Doctor Zhivago*; Lara and Yurii

The opening of the novel

Part 1 of *Doctor Zhivago* opens somewhere in the Russian countryside in 1902. In this chapter I shall try to draw out certain modes of feeling and behaving introduced in it, as well as the view of history expressed there, all of which are important for understanding the whole novel.

The title of Part 1 is 'The Five O'Clock Express'. It starts, however, with people surging forward not in a train but in a funeral procession:

They were walking and walking and singing 'Eternal Memory' and, each time they stopped, this seemed to go on being sung just as before by feet and horses and breaths of wind.

The first word of the book is *Shli*: 'They were walking'. Impersonal, anonymous, communal, without a pronoun, it flows easily into the notion of the hymn's continuation in the surroundings. The sentence could be read either as a slightly quaint beginning to an ordinary realistic story; or one might dwell on the sense of a more than realistic quality in it, some special meaning in the singing of feet and horses. Following this, we might, without feeling compelled to, see something symbolic in the way passers-by join in the procession — anyone can be part of this movement (and the novel will be full of random characters, passers-by as it were, joining in its story) — as well as in the way the name 'Zhivago' is introduced: it too is communal, or non-individual, for it makes 'no difference' whose name, whose burial, this is.

'Who's being buried?' 'Zhivago', was the answer. 'That's why, then. So that's it.' 'No, not him. Her.' 'No difference. Rest in peace. A rich funeral.'

Furthermore, the name has a meaning and its place in the implied sentence invites the reader to attend to it. A literal translation of the Russian would be: 'Whom are they burying?' and since *zhiv* means 'alive' and *-ago* indicates an accusative masculine adjective, the answer could read: 'They are burying the living person.'

The words of the psalm which are quoted in the next paragraph are surely a motto for the book, as they come right at its beginning, and they too are very much about living and flourishing: 'The earth is the Lord's and the fulness thereof, the world and those who dwell therein.' The script of the film based on *Doctor Zhivago* undermined Pasternak's purpose when it replaced these affirmative words with the negative 'Now is life's artful triumph of vanities destroyed', as the American editions of the book undermined it by replacing 'eternal memory' with 'eternal rest'. Nothing could be less apt as a motto than destruction and repose. The novel may start with a funeral but its entire tendency will be to counteract the funereal.

Images of life and death are subtly juxtaposed in this opening description. Next to the earth's 'fulness' is the 'terrible rushing' to fill in the grave with that same earth; then the mound of earth is climbed by a ten-year-old boy, whose name, we guess, also is 'the living', to weep and be lashed by heavy rain as his mother has just been lashed by a rain of clods. A lightly suggested allegory develops: life mourns its own burial. Meanwhile, set against that, the whole movement of this section (1:1) is first towards, then away from, the graveyard. Its framing phrases, 'eternal memory' at the beginning and 'away from the graveyard' at the end, hint at two different ways of surmounting death. Then a single fact is given about the boy's uncle who leads him away: he is 'a priest unfrocked at his own request'. His name, Vedenyapin, starts with a syllable which occurs in Russian words for both knowledge and guidance, and we may surmise that what guides life away from death is a knowledge which used to be, but no longer is, the preserve of priests. Vedenyapin will turn out to be the propounder of a new form of Christianity and an influence on his nephew and other main personages of the book.

The word 'allegory' may not be wholly apt. It is not the case that everything in the narrative is contrived to stand for something in some second order of truth. Rather, our attention is drawn to certain meaningful configurations of experience, and the accompanying names and facts can often be interpreted so as to confirm them. Two such configurations arising from the opening section have to do with overcoming death and with not making speeches. Both are connected with the boy Yurii, or Yura. The first is developed in the next section (1:2). Here he and his uncle stay at a monastery (which, like so many places in the novel, is within hearing of a railway); again there is a lashing by the weather when the blizzard attacks acacias and cabbages and heaps the new grave with snow; and again the boy is seized by distress and is led out of it by his uncle. Straight after this we learn that, being the son of a once famous, now ruined millionaire, he has memories of a time when all sorts of products bore the name 'Zhivago' and you could be driven far off to a fairyland where, in a quiet park, 'crows settled on downhanging branches of fir trees' and 'their cawing sounded out cracklingly like the splitting branch of a tree'.

The comparison, crossing animal with vegetable, is abrupt yet evocative, and so is the whole description – perceptually and emotionally precise and rich, yet curtailed, ending suddenly at the very moment when enough has been said: the park, the crows with their branch-like sound, then the vividly observed running of dogs, lights going on, evening, and the recollection is finished. No conclusion is drawn, no psychological point is made, and there is practically no convenient linking up with what comes next. Passages like this will occur throughout the novel; a mosaic of prose poems, or proto-poems, is worked into its texture.

The story continues with the boy going a year later with his uncle to a country estate where, in another quiet park, he is again overwhelmed, this time by a heat-haze instead of a blizzard, and here for the third time he goes through both grief

over death and recovery from it: he thinks of his mother,
swoons, prays and comes round in a state of unusual
'lightness'. Now overcoming death becomes a *leitmotif*
accompanying Yurii. The funeral in Part 3 is important in this
respect, as during the church service there he realises he has
grown into a relation of equality with the whole universe and
is 'at home' in it. Because of this, when the other mourners
lag behind after the burial, he is able to walk rapidly ahead,
away from the grave, starting to compose a poem and reflect-
ing that 'art has two constant, two unending preoccupations:
it is always meditating on death and thereby always creating
life'.

The second pattern of behaviour to be identified in the
opening is what I have called 'not making a speech'. This not-
doing is the very first thing we see Yurii do. He climbs onto
the mound, and the author comments: 'Only somebody in the
numb and feelingless state which generally comes at the end
of a big funeral could suppose the boy wished to make an
address on his mother's grave.' The sentence is disconcertingly tentative: does anyone suppose it? Through its oddness,
its having a paragraph to itself and its being rendered irrelevant by the next paragraph where the boy merely bursts into
sobs, it gives a strangely oblique prominence to his not
making any address or speech.

In *Doctor Zhivago* some characters make speeches and
others do not. Speech-making is presented as unnatural and
'false' and is connected with a fundamental loss of personality in the twentieth century. There are numerous examples:
Tsar Nicholas surprisingly omits to intone the usual pom-
posities about 'My Nation' when he visits the front. War
journalists, however, pour forth clichés and rhetoric at a fast
rate. Lieutenant Gintz, in Part 5, is lynched for his speechify-
ing. Yurii is continually feeling stifled by the speech-making
of others (the deaf-mute, the partisans' leader Liverii, the
dealers in clichés such as 'dawn of the future', 'torchbearers
of mankind') (9:7). And in a small but important episode in
Part 8 the incident at the opening of the book is echoed. Here
the Zhivago family have arrived at Torfyanaya, last stop

on their long journey to Varykino, and are astonished by the quietness of the provincial station 'hidden in a birchgrove' with birdsong and swaying treetops (8:7). For Yurii's wife Tonya it brings a lull in the noise of events, a moment of clarity. Now as her 'eyes and ears suddenly open' to the surroundings she abandons a speech she has mentally prepared, every anxious, mistrustful, indignant word of which the author nonetheless recounts, as something *not* said. Instead of all that, she exclaims 'How lovely!' and bursts into tears. Yura in Part 1 wept for grief, Tonya in Part 8 weeps for joy, but the two moments are alike in their putting weeping in place of speech-making, and preferring new emotion to old phrases.

Eleven-year-old Yura's recovery from his swoon in a state of well-being and lightness is the last we hear of him for a very long time. He is displaced by two other boys. First is Misha Gordon, travelling on the five o'clock express distantly visible from the estate and worrying about his Jewishness as well as about an alcoholic who, after showing him kindness, has leapt from the train to his death. Our attention switches from Misha to the suicide. Learning that it is that of a former millionaire, we may guess it is Yurii's father (the translator unwarrantedly puts this in) happening to die near the very house where his son is staying. Thus centrally in Part 1 stands this huge coincidence and crossing of fate's paths. Along with it, as yet unidentifiable, is a mass of material for future coincidences. The widow Tiverzina, for example, one of the crowd that gathers when the train is stopped, will turn out to be complexly connected with the main characters of the novel: her son is the work-mate of the railwayman Antipov, whose son, in turn, will later marry Lara, with whom Yurii is to fall in love. The callous lawyer at the same scene, who is partly responsible for the death, will be Lara's seducer and thus a force for destruction in connection with both main characters.

The third boy, Nika Dudorov, goes through a heady illusion of power in the same park where Yurii prays: 'If God exists, I am He', thinks Nika. He too recalls his mother and has an infancy memory which mingles animal and vegetable: in a far-off Georgian courtyard was an unusual tree with 'leaves like elephant's ears'. The nature of these comparisons (which John Wain has called 'barrier-crumbling similes') is here carefully drawn to our attention, for Nika 'could not get used to the idea that it was a plant and not an animal'. Unlike Yurii, Nika is full of youthful rebellion and resentments; he quarrels with a girl he has taken out in a boat and they fall into the lake; Part 1 ends deep in the emotions of this boy who is not going to have much importance in the novel and to whose character this episode will have no relevance whatever.

Why these three boys and why the emphasis on boyhood, in a novel not concerned with psychological development? *Doctor Zhivago* was originally to be entitled 'Boys and Girls', and throughout the novel so many male characters are very young that a message seems implied: of tolerance, or hope. But in Part 1 Pasternak is saying something about human likeness and vocational difference. Yurii's fate crosses Misha's, his early memories resemble Nika's. But Misha's 'mainspring remained a feeling of anxiety', just the opposite of Yurii's experience of lightness, and Nika's game of being 'God' is just the opposite of Yurii's praying. Misha and Nika are assertive, militant boys, preoccupied by psychological dilemmas, the kind of thing this novel is not going to be about, while Yurii is passive, receptive and not at all bent on defining himself. Like Nika, he goes through an enchantment and a fall in a paradisal garden, but whereas Nika himself playfully 'enchants' a tree, Yurii responds to an enchantment around him; and whereas Nika's fall is due to his own aggression, Yurii's is from surrender to a feeling that seems to come from outside. There is a sustained contrast of active and receptive. Indeed, most of what happens to the boy Yurii is, or can be, expressed in passive or intransitive verbs: he is led from the grave, he is helped, he weeps, swoons, wakes. An exception is that when snow covers his mother's grave he longs 'to do something' but doesn't know what — doesn't *yet* know

what, we will say when we have read on to a later funeral and
find him beginning to write. Even before reading on, we
know from the Contents list that Yurii is to be not only a
doctor, but a poet. What is distinctive, then, in the childhood
of the poet is this emotional and yielding openness to the
immediate environment.

In Part 1 there are two passages of philosophical statement
which are linked to the motifs and patterns noted so far:
Vedenyapin's remarks about history, and a paragraph starting 'All the movements in the world . . .'

Both statements are offered with authority. The second,
while just construable as Misha's indirect thought, is more
plausibly that of the author or narrator; and Vedenyapin's
remarks are made to someone who cannot object because he
does not 'understand a word', as will again be the case in Part
2, when he explains his ideas to the obtuse Tolstoyan. In fact,
much of the novel's dialogue in which ideas are set out is
quasi-monologue: either the two speakers are in complete
agreement, or else only one speaks and the other's disagree-
ment is briefly alluded to. (Another kind of dialogue, the
rhythmic and purposeless talk between minor characters, will
be discussed in chapter 6.)

Not only are Vedenyapin's ideas not contradicted, they are
preceded by authorial praise of him, almost in the form of a
testimonial: among the dogmatic philosophers of his time, he
alone 'moved ahead', was no hypocrite and 'thirsted for the
new'. Something similar is subsequently done for his nephew,
who 'thought well and wrote very well'. Such programmatic
recommendations suggest that Pasternak felt uneasy either
about his readers – were they clever or sympathetic enough
to listen to his message and identify its bearers? – or else
about his medium: how could this unfamiliar vehicle, the
novel, with its frightening directness, carry something he is
used to saying in the more subtly distilled modes of poetry?
Of course, the testimonials are not needed. Echoes of
Vedenyapin's thought continue to the end, supported by all
the book's imagery and structure.

First he says that the fault of contemporary philosophers is their herding together and swearing allegiance to fixed doctrines, whereas truth is sought only by individuals. The date is 1903 but the relevance to later times is obvious. There is nothing we should be loyal to, says Vedenyapin, except 'immortality, which is another word for life'. He explains his philosophy of history:

it is possible to be an atheist . . . and yet to know that the human being doesn't live in nature but in history, and that history, as we understand it today, was founded by Christ and the Gospels are its basis. And what *is* history? It is the setting up, through the ages, of works that are consistently devoted to the solving of death and to the overcoming of it in the future. For the sake of this, mathematical infinity and electromagnetic waves are discovered and symphonies are written.

According to this rather strange and spiritual view of history – quite opposed to Marxism, which regards history as centuries of class struggle for the control of material goods – a second universe, coherent and habitable, is built up over the centuries by human creative work, using energies inspired by the gospels: love, 'the idea of free personality' and 'the idea of life as sacrifice'. The contrast with the ancient world, which lacked these ideas or energies, and with Roman civilisation in particular, is developed in later ponderings of Vedenyapin's, as well as in Sima Tuntseva's belief that with the birth of Christ 'something shifted in the world – there was an end to Rome . . . leaders and nations were replaced by personality'. The precariousness of 'history' is emphasised: if we didn't always have it, we could lose it again, and the suggestion is that in our century it is being lost. Yet while it is there, it is neither inward nor elsewhere, but lying around us like a landscape, 'more closely than earth and sky', so that now the human being 'dies not on the road under a fence but at home in history, dies at the height of labours devoted to overcoming death'.

While Vedenyapin is saying this, the elder Zhivago is dying not at the height of creative labours but in drunkenness and despair on a railway embankment, virtually on a road under

a fence. We don't know enough about him to say he dies outside history, we can as yet only note it as some kind of cor-
roboration. Much later a second roadside death (that of his
son) will be described as part of the larger coherence of
things.

The authorial passage starting 'All movements in the
world . . .' supports Vedenyapin's philosophy by stating that
happiness is possible because lives are interconnected through
a 'supreme and fundamental unconcern', which arises from
a sense that everything takes place 'not only on the earth
where the dead are interred but also in something else'.
Wordsworth's 'sense sublime / Of something far more deeply
interfused' may come to mind. But the translators, not
trusting the indefinite 'something else', expanded it to
'another level' or (in American editions) 'another region'.
Such levels and regions are alien to our author, who merely
adds that the 'something else' has been called by various
names, including 'Kingdom of God' and (again) 'history'.
'History' is of course no conventional alternative to
'Kingdom of God'. The Church has a long tradition of seeing
earthly history and Heaven as distinct from each other, while
Marxists are unlikely to interchange the two terms. But the
idea of the interchangeability of labels and the carefree way
of treating it are both important here. The style is at once
earnest and weightless, as though any heaviness would alter
what is said. In fact Vedenyapin is always made to speak
impromptu, 'while his thoughts were still alive', and every
restatement of his or related ideas is described as spontaneous
and unpremeditated, so that what may appear to be a set
speech is not one. Lightness – a quality of the boy Yurii, and
also attributed by Vedenyapin to Christ – is another word
for the supreme unconcern that holds people together. At
Yurii's coffin, Lara will recall the 'freedom and unconcern'
that always emanated from him, qualities which belong to the
'gift for living'.

In a conversation about his novel, Pasternak once said –
lightly – 'I used religious symbolism to give warmth to the
book. Now some critics have become so wrapped up in those

symbols – which are put in the book the way stoves go into a house, to warm it up – that they would like me to commit myself and climb into the stove.' It is tempting to point out that a house can hardly be lived in without a stove to warm it, but one doesn't need to be a Christian to grasp the idea of history as a home. Much of the book is about the return to 'prehistory', the loss of the sense of home; much is about brief recoveries of it; all is imbued with the hope of recreating it.

Lara and Yurii

The milieu in Part 1 was that of professors, lawyers, liberal industrialists, revolutionary aristocrats and ruined millionaires. Part 2, set in Moscow, introduces small business people and railway workers and managers. As in most of the novel, there is a large number of incidental characters, some of them appearing for the first time, some harking back to the stopped train scene, some to reappear fleetingly. Against this background of many interweaving or coinciding lives, and among the strikes, marches and fighting of 1905, the story is told of the seduction of a schoolgirl, Lara, by the rich lawyer, Komarovsky. It is told entirely through their separate reflections on it.

Because of her humiliation, Lara sympathises with the demonstrators and street barricaders, and justifies the workers' strikes to her mother (at the same time connecting their liberation with 'Christ's opinion' – making us recall Vedenyapin's philosophy). But before we sum her up as a rebellious victim of the old social order or of unscrupulous male lust, we must note features that do not fit this picture. In at least two ways the victim stereotype is avoided. For one thing, while loathing the sexual adventure she also enjoys it and, though disgusted with the relationship, she gives Komarovsky a 'sly wink of complicity' just when her mother has nearly committed suicide over it. And it is worth noting that there is a corresponding evasion of the villain stereotype in the depiction of Komarovsky. Lara later calls him a 'wellbred animal' and a 'monster of mediocrity' and we have seen his involvement in the suicide in Part 1, yet he is shown to feel for her a more than sensual admiration, finding her hands 'astonishing, as a lofty form of thought may be astonishing'; and at the end, though he is said to have ruined her life, he will turn up in an ambiguously benevolent role.

For another thing, there is such generality in the accounts of Lara that she not only misses representing a type but avoids being an individual too. Both the detail of her inner thoughts and the external descriptions of her are designed to 'efface' any particularity. She lies in bed and sees herself, from within, as extending from left shoulder to right toe. It is the awareness of being a human body, a finite piece of matter − not a condition peculiar to Lara. Moreover, 'left shoulder' crops up six or seven times in the novel (an example is quoted on page 94) as if with some legendary or general significance. When she is seen from outside, walking along a street for instance, the description swerves away from individuality and concreteness: 'Lara walked rapidly. Some kind of force carried her, as if she were striding on air, a proud animating force' (2:19). We could compare this sentence with one in which Tolstoy describes Anna Karenina's gait: 'She walked rapidly, carrying her rather full figure with extraordinary lightness.' There is as much use of abstraction here and nearly as much suggestion of a proud animating force: but we *see* Anna Karenina in the act of walking, while we do not see Lara.

Inner causality, or motivation, is a feature of the traditional novel which Pasternak wished to replace with something else and which is in fact conspicuously absent from *Zhivago*. If we ask what it is in Anna Karenina that enables her so warmly to press Dolly to forgive her husband his infidelity, we shall find ourselves understanding a good deal about these three characters as well as about the whole patterning of that novel. If we ask why Raskolnikov kills the old woman in *Crime and Punishment*, the many answers we get are all illuminating. But if we ask why, in terms of psychological make-up or pressure of circumstances, one of

Pasternak's characters undertakes this or that action, we are likely to get nowhere. Let us look at Part 3 for examples.

Lara conceives the idea of shooting Komarovsky when her brother begs her to get money from him. Why doesn't he suggest she get it from her rich benefactor, Kologrivov, from whom she does in fact get it? Later she wants to repay Kologrivov and decides (having practised with the revolver) that she will now ask Komarovsky for the money and shoot him if he refuses. How can she be so ready to murder a man, years after he has stopped harming her and she has got free of him? Perhaps she wishes to test his ability to be honourable and generous? But why? Or has she been harbouring the desire to kill him all these years (unknown to the reader) and the request for money, which she expects him to refuse, is to be a pretext? But why seek a pretext when she has the courage, the hatred and the gun? And why expect him to refuse? In order to follow her plan, she gatecrashes a happy Christmas party. Surely this is both terribly selfish and unnecessarily dangerous? Why not shoot him when he's alone? Nothing in the text even prompts this question. It's as if everything must be, or might as well be, just as it is. At the party she sees Komarovsky playing cards and realises he is *not* seducing another girl as once he seduced her. Does this lessen her wish to shoot him? She notices with interest that sitting with him is a lawyer called Kornakov who once made a fanatical speech at the sentencing of some insurgent railwaymen, one of whom was her friend Pasha's father. Lara fires the gun. At whom? She has not tried to find out whether Komarovsky will give her the money. Does she decide to kill Kornakov on the spur of the moment either to avenge Pasha's father or because he represents an oppressive society? Or does she fire at Kornakov and Komarovsky together, not caring whom she hits, in general revolt against sexual and political oppression? We get a page and a half of Komarovsky's feelings about the matter, but not a word about hers or her motives. Nor is any mystery made about it, no hint that it would be of interest to know what she had in mind. After this Lara accepts any amount of help from

Komarovsky, the man she decided to kill, and a lot more money from Kologrivov, although it was unease about owing him money that started her off on the path of murder. After her marriage she even invites Komarovsky to her farewell party as an old friend. Why? Not only has she recently planned, and perhaps tried, to kill him, but her new husband has just gone through immense suffering on learning of her relationship with him. How is it Komarovsky can expect, as he does, to be welcome at their new home in the Urals?

None of these questions has an answer. On the level of cause and effect, all is unclear and implausible. We have to look for other kinds of meaning. One kind of meaning is symbolic. The shooting signifies Lara's affinity with 'the boys shooting' that she admired in 1905, with the future Strelnikov and with the spirit of the times — she is contrasted with Tonya in that she belongs to times of danger, change and revolt. Her accepting help from Komarovsky, keeping him in her life, may suggest an unbreakable link between seduced and seducer and, more clearly, symbolises the dependence of beauty on the common, lowly conditions of existence. 'Beauty is always in chains', Pasternak has written. Later in the novel, Yurii twice talks about jealousy, saying he would not be jealous of a rival who was his equal, but he is jealous of Komarovsky as he is of the air, of time and of his beloved's illnesses.

Another meaning is that motives are not, in this author's view, what people are most significantly moved by. We do not act on reasoned decisions and definable inner promptings; relationships are no longer to be seen as consistent patterns of cause and effect. Instead we live in a trance of interconnections. In *A Safe Conduct* Pasternak wrote that 'our most innocent hallos and goodbyes would have no meaning at all, were time not threaded through with the unity of life's events — that is, with the criss-crossing effects of the trance of the everyday', and he is still concerned with this in *Zhivago*. What comes next in the farewell party episode is in fact a trance. After a series of remarkably unmotivated actions, including taking apart a meat-mincer (or is she

dreaming of mincing up – or of not mincing up – Komarovsky, the man of flesh?), Lara falls into a hypnotic state, looking out of her kitchen window, and becomes deeply absorbed
in the yard and a hobbled horse that has strayed there.
Nothing could be more irrelevant to the story or more relevant to the novel's message and vision. (This hobbled horse
will be discussed in chapter 6.)

Lara is an image of vitality, sexual and revolutionary, yet
more expansive, more elusive than either. 'Turbulent',
'rebellious', 'striding', are the adjectives that describe her.
So, however, is 'harmonious', and, later on, 'domestic',
'maternal', 'practical'. But for all his unquestioning tradi-
tionality about gender roles (the later Lara is forever washing
and ironing, shaking out carpets, nursing, caring for her
child), the author is not particularly concerned with them. He
is interested in the speed, movement and strength that may
inform any human being, the 'proud' force that can animate
the piece of finite matter; and with the way it seems especially
present in some people and in everything they do; what they
touch grows wings. Lara is one of those people. She represents the energies that are referred to in such ideas as that of
a 'wingedly material thought' (1:4), or of 'the commonplace
touched by genius' (9:7). Another word used of her (by the
author) is 'pure' – 'the purest creature on earth'. This has
nothing to do with her sexual life but means, as the context
makes clear, she is no theoriser or speech-maker and is not
cluttered by 'premature abstractions'. Instead, she exists to
'make sense of the crazy beauty of the earth and to call
everything by its name'. Feeling precedes utterance.

This order of experiencing is not exclusive to Lara. We
have seen it in Tonya and it is also typical of Yurii. When
Pasternak wrote that rather than delineate characters he
wished to 'efface' them, he meant, I suggest, something to do
with this sharing of qualities and experiences. Not particular
idiosyncrasies, not whole, rounded, psychological make-ups
interested him, but that which joined each individual to
humanity. Erotic, parental and compassionate love; worship and admiration; the need to feel untrammelled; delight

in the world both as a whole and in its detail; pleasure in human creative works and in tradition, pleasure also in innovation and change; and the sense (perhaps more than any other in this book) of location, of being somewhere, and of being at home — these things, besieged by hostile and divisive forces, are shared by the main group of characters, almost as though a single subjectivity were parcelled out provisionally among them, something like a communal awareness or, better, a set of overlapping consciousnesses.

Pasternak seems to have had this sort of thing in mind when he wrote to Jacqueline de Proyart in 1958, in French: 'Should we simply love one another, or should we love what is immortal in us, the only thing that counts?' 'Immortal': this word, of central importance to Vedenyapin and applicable to what he means by 'free personality', recalls a talk Pasternak once gave, as a young student of philosophy, on the subject of 'Symbolism and Immortality'. Subjectivity, he then said, is a property not of the individual but of the human race; a portion of this undying subjectivity, with which we participate in history, remains from each one of us at our death. The corollary — that there is a sense in which we do not die — links further with the philosophy of immortality in *Zhivago*. Thus Yurii (unprepared, surprised at himself) tells Tonya's mother, Anna Gromeko, when she is ill that she need not worry about resurrection, because: 'You in others, this is your soul' — which could seem a platitude but for its combination with the theory of consciousness which he also spontaneously expounds. Consciousness is like the headlamps of an engine — catastrophic if turned inward but excellent for lighting up the way ahead, the surroundings of the journey. Not my introspective self, then, but the world as I have perceived and known it, is what will continue in those who survive me. It might be said that *Zhivago* is all about just this: the world lit up by many minds — a whole world (no modernist's fragmentations) lit up by joined and sharing minds. Yurii's talk to Anna contains his version of the statement about happiness and unconcern in Part 1, his way of trying to speak of an elusively proceeding coherence in the universe.

In simpler form, it becomes the main statement of his poem 'Wedding'. A particularly clear instance of shared minds is the scene in Part 13 where Sima Tuntseva explains her ideas about the Bible in the hearing of Yurii and Lara, each of whom, sitting in separate rooms, silently agrees with all she says, and it is of no importance that she herself is virtually characterless and unimportant to the novel's plot: her name and patronymic, Serafima Severinovna, suggesting 'seraph of the north', may be enough said about her, along with the fact that most people consider her crazy. She, Yurii, Lara and (through his influence) Vedenyapin constitute at this point a single consciousness.

But instances abound, for this is the dominant factor in the depiction of the main characters. It is, further, very telling that although there is much talk of cruel, cliché-ridden, speech-making or unoriginal people − the lament about them runs through the whole book − such people are depicted only fleetingly. It would seem that all persons, when you look at them closely, do participate in the general coherence of the world, while what fights against it is not persons but a force of evil sometimes working through them. Our author does not say this. But when he presents those who are supposed to be villains or in error, he states their fault in abstract terms − they are exploiters, or rigid servants of principle, or blind to the truth, or only ever preparing to live − yet the concrete person comes over as attractive. We have seen this in the case of Komarovsky − who, notably, has a friend called Satanidi, which suggests that the satanic accompanies him as a separate entity, without being identified with him. Liverii, the leader of the Partisans, though supposed to have all the wrong ideas and though told by Yurii that he can go to the devil for having sold his soul to the logic that leads to bloodshed, comes across as a likeable, enthusiastic youth. Pamfil Palykh, who slaughters his family, is presented as pitiable, while his monstrous face links him not only with the scar-faced thief at Lara's party, but with the legendary Bacchus of Anna Gromeko's reminiscence − a folktale ogre? a sheer force of badness? All the book's characters are, as individuals, either likeable or forgivable, and at the same time each is related to something other than individual, some force or tradition or universal meaning. Idiosyncrasies are played down in the central group of characters and it would be no easy task to give a character sketch of any of them; it is almost impossible to do it for Tonya, her mother or her father, and quite impossible for the children, Sasha and Katya. But the different forms taken, in Lara and in Yurii, by the shared energy and the shared 'way of sensing the world' − *mirooshchushchenie* in Russian − are fully explored. Perhaps one could say that in Lara they take the form of *élan vital*, sheer movement and vitality, along with great caring, love of people and of work. In Yurii they take the form of artistic creation.

Even less is said of Yurii's looks than of Lara's. He has a snub nose and is plain: these facts are mentioned twice, but are given no importance at all. We are not invited to see him. But how he sees the world is fully shown to us. The emphasis is in fact upon the seeing. The impressionability, or receptivity, that is associated with him in Part 1 continues to be stressed. It is stressed through such information as that his dissertation concerns the physiology of the eye or that, as a doctor, he excels in diagnosis − sees at a glance what is wrong (as he will also see what is rotten in the state of Russia). It is stressed in other ways too. Visions come to Yurii in the forest of the Civil War. And there is the emphatically visual quality of his very first encounters with Lara, the two intense glimpses before they become acquainted. The first is the conclusion of Part 2. All opportunity for emotional drama, and there was plenty, has been studiously avoided; then at the very end comes this one episode of silent observation, a defining scene that is both theatrical and actionless. Through a doorway, at the Guichards' hotel, Yurii (an adolescent cultivating a belief in chastity) catches sight of two people deep in a private sexual drama. What he sees is called a 'dumb scene', a 'puppet show', 'lit as if by footlights'; and other theatrical terms are used, so that he is cast as absolute spectator. The scene appears meant for him, for it is calling to him 'for help' (the translators quite wrongly substituted 'helpless') and more strongly than ever he feels the demand on him to do something: 'what was Yurii to do?' Perhaps this is a version of the question 'what is to be done?' that reverberates through the Russian nineteenth century (and was used as a title by Tolstoy, Chernyshevsky and Lenin). *Doctor Zhivago* may be seen as structured by this question. For, years later, Strelnikov will be astounded to learn that Yurii's first glimpse of Lara corresponded to his own, though this led him to become a revolutionary. 'You saw the same thing?' he asks. 'And what did you do about it?' Between the two questions: 'What was he to do?' and 'What did you do?' lies a lifetime's answer.

The second pre-acquaintance glimpse Yurii has of Lara is at the second interrupted party, after she has fired the gun: 'that same girl!' Again he is all observation and she all action. Subsequently, he drifts into marriage, gets sent to war service, is injured and is brought by chance to meet Lara. She, by contrast, has been living actively: marrying the man of her choice, and setting off in search of him in the war. She is working as a nurse when Yurii turns up in her life — not as a doctor, we note, but as a patient.

After the Revolution both of them move to the east of Russia, Lara returning there purposefully, Yurii being passively taken there by his family. The Zhivago family's departure is preceded by a short section (7:1) which seems designed to put conclusive emphasis on Yurii's lack of any desire or power to manipulate his fate. (We recall too how his wife was chosen for him by, so to speak, the sheer force of proximity, confirmed by Anna Gromeko's decisiveness.) For his inconsequential reluctance to go to Varykino is made as pointless as possible, by being placed after the family's reasonable arguments for going. Moreover, even after the statement that they did in fact go, his objections to the journey, covering a page and a half and amounting to a whole numbered section, are prefaced by his saying that he intends to give in and go. The uncritical thoroughness with which they are expounded (like the thorough account of the speech

Tonya later thinks of making, but does not make, at the Torfyanaya station — see page 52f.) suggests that his ineffectuality is no fault, and that such indecisiveness, the to-and-fro of hesitation before one is drawn into some happening, is as valid a part of reality, as worthy to be traced out in all its detail, as are actions and decisions. Here, as in many other places, the novel tacitly works against the over-tidy and clear-cut picture of history presented by Marxism. We have also to bear in mind that Yurii's hesitations and tendency to submit to whatever life may bring — the 'characterlessness' he at one point is said to worry about in himself — are but one aspect of him; its obverse is the adamant clarity of the artist at work.

When he and Lara meet, again by chance, in Yuryatin, he is once again the observer, looking up from his book in the library, and she is being an active influence upon somebody in the reading-room. Their love affair starts with a scene that is well designed to concentrate in itself the allegory of seeing and acting. Having learned Lara's address and gone to her house, Yurii catches sight of her in her yard as she fetches water from a well; the sight — the seeing — is complicated by a sudden whirlwind and cloud of dust. When this disperses, he sees her:

With the yoke on her left shoulder . . . pressing between her knees the billowing lower part of her house-coat . . . she was about to move to the house with the water but had stopped, held up by a new gust of wind which tore the scarf from her head, started tousling her hair and carried the scarf to the far end of the fence, to the still clucking hens.
(9:13)

So much here is typical of Pasternak's methods: the extension of the description into the impersonal environment (as once wind and horses joined in the singing of a funeral hymn, so now the hens join in the ruffling of the woman); the portrayal of a person not for how she looks but for how she is affected by wind and weather; that she is experienced as beautiful is a matter not of features but of movement and interrelation with her surroundings; also, here is an example of the frequent association of Lara with water. But I wish to point especially to the fact that what for Lara is a moment of struggle and activity is for Yurii a complex moment of witnessing

Yurii Zhivago is not so much a 'character' with individual voice, appearance and habits as the representative of a certain way of being, in which the main thing to note, perhaps, is the tendency to happiness. Yurii's many transports of joy (often amid hardship and pain) may start with love, for a woman or for nature, but they issue in gratitude for existence: 'How sweet it is to exist! How sweet to live in the world and to love life!' Although Pasternak referred far more often to Tolstoy, the existential Dostoevsky is closer to him here. Markel, the brother of Zosima in *The Brothers Karamazov*, approaches death in a state of bliss because he has woken up to the realisation that 'life is Paradise and we are all in Paradise, it's just that we don't want to know it'. (Pasternak may have remembered this when he gave one of his characters the unusual name 'Markel'.) 'Beauty will save the world' wrote Dostoevsky in another context, and in Varykino (14:14) Yurii notes that art serves beauty, beauty is the happiness of possessing form, everything must possess form in order to exist, therefore 'art, including tragic art, is the story of the happiness of existence'.

Chapter 5

Yurii Zhivago and the Revolution; Strelnikov and others; coincidences

It is symptomatic of Pasternak's method that both the 1917 revolutions, which most Soviet novels present through crowd scenes with noise, speeches and collective excitement, are reflected by him in the response of one man hearing the news from afar.

At the time of the February Revolution, Yurii is away on war service in Melyuzeev. Like Pasternak himself, he will look back with nostalgia to the summer of 1917, the period between the revolutions, when 'everyone went mad in their own way, and each one's life existed in its own right, not to explain or illustrate the rightness of some higher policy'. Part 5 of the novel is devoted to the madness and individualities of that exceptional time. During it, Yurii tells Lara his feelings: 'the roof has been ripped off Russia — we're out under the open sky' (5:8). He says nothing about the monarchy, the Provisional Government, the Soviets, the violence in Petrograd, or conflicting ideologies. Instead, he talks of the change in the quality of existence, the sheer experience of what it feels like for an entire country to be altered by a political event: 'Freedom dropping down out of the blue . . . Freedom by accident, by a misunderstanding. And how huge everyone is and bewildered.' 'Out of the blue', or a similar phrase, is used by Yurii of other things too, especially of genius, birth and (quoting Tyutchev) the coming of summer. The deliberately plain idiom is chosen as the vehicle of something supremely valuable, the 'waking up' of the human being, the perceiving of existence itself. The unexpected and insistent 'by a misunderstanding' (or, 'by mistake') is a recurrent motif which will be discussed in the next chapter. Here it is almost equivalent to 'spontaneously': freedom from those plans and decisions that don't admit or allow mistakes, inadvertencies, freedom from being subsumed under any official plan. A vision of communality is also an essential feature of Yurii's response to the February Revolution. As in a fairy-tale (he uses fairy-tale language) the very environment is joining in:

Mother Russia has shifted from the spot, she can't keep still, can't stop walking, can't stop talking. And not only people — stars and trees have come together, they're talking away to one another, nocturnal flowers have begun to philosophise, stone buildings are holding meetings.

Exhilarated by events, Yurii falls in love, and so nearly declares it that the ironing-board begins to burn. This is narrated realistically enough — Lara has left the board to approach him — but as usual there is the possibility of allegory: everything is set on fire, changed, by love and by history.

What Yurii says to his guests in Moscow later that summer is not what he said in Melyuzeev, and is even incompatible with it. Then, he spoke of the sea of socialism and great flow of life; now, in Moscow, he speaks of a sea of blood set flowing by the war which is bound to reach everyone, and 'the Revolution is this flood'. It is later, there has been more bloodshed, he has doubtless come to new thoughts. But what is more important is that Yurii does not assume an obligation to make his thoughts or his feelings consistent, he is never setting up a theory or a philosophy (and says as much when going 'back to nature' in Varykino), but is always trying to catch, in images and other expressions, something of the unique quality of each moment.

At the Moscow gathering he again eschews analysis and instead makes predictions — of confusion, horror, an end to personal life, and finally a completely new order in Russia in which the past will have been forgotten. His listeners, like Vedenyapin's, understand nothing. Then, the new life and the catastrophe which is to precede it, as well as the impossibility of being articulate about it and the silliness of the guests' smoky chatter, are all symbolised in the crashes of thunder. These fresh sounds, wonderfully compared to potatoes being turned up from a vegetable plot, coincide with the opening of a window and reveal the true 'ingredients of existence: water and air, the desire for joy, earth and sky'. From now on Yurii feels sure that he and his class are doomed.

His Moscow speech, which is his one piece of speech-making (significantly enough attempted while drunk), makes implicit allusion to the Book of Revelation, the last book of the Bible which, he once said, all great art continues. 'Revelation' is a fearful account of vengeance, plagues, devastation, seas of blood, death upon death (hence the connotation its Greek name, Apocalypse, has come to have, of final and total catastrophe). It issues, however, in a vision of the New Jerusalem, a new order of things in which 'there will be no more death' − Yurii quotes these words to Anna Gromeko on her sickbed. The whole Bible culminates in the vision of no more death. How is 'all great art' to be understood as continuing it? And is *Doctor Zhivago* to be read as doing so? Hints of a new Moscow at the end of the novel support such a reading, which might be based on two senses of 'continue'. First, it takes up the story where the other leaves off: it shows within the real, ordinary, well-known world, with all its deaths and burials, an already infinite sprouting of deathless resurrectional moments. A cemetery is walked away from, a child is born, a tyrant is toppled, a poem is composed, a girl escapes from subjection; someone falls in love, overhears a song, recovers from illness, is rapt by a vision. A long linkage of these moments, with light emphasis upon them, goes through the novel. In the second sense, it continues seeing the world as the Prophet, John the Divine, did, applying to modern history that ancient invocation of catastrophe. This certainly underlies Yurii's inebriate predictions, for although he looks ahead to a wholly new life − Russia 'the first kingdom of socialism' (an interesting paradox) − his chief theme is the horror of the time which must precede that, and in which 'it will seem to us that there is nothing any more but killing and dying'.

These prophecies do not diminish his response to the Revolution in October, which is again affirmative, but not in the same way as was his response to the February events. This time he is talking to himself. Alexander Gromeko is present but is not listening and not needed. The February event was experienced as something akin to himself, the October one is welcome but alien. Yurii reads the news bulletin while alone in a blizzard (at the very moment that, as yet unrecognised, down from above and out into the snow walks the man who is to protect him in future political blizzards, his half-brother Evgraf). February brought passion, October brings contemplation. Yurii quietly admires the Bolsheviks' first decrees and discerns 'genius' in their ruthless directness: only genius dare burst like this into the midst of everyday life.

It is instructive to compare the metaphors he uses for the two revolutions. In the first, people all over the country are visualised as becoming taller as though a roof were raised and they became able to stand straight or to grow. For the second, the metaphor is not an upward but a downward one: the surgeon's knife striking in to an inert body, a mechanical invasion of an organic process but represented in the most beneficial form this can take, a doctor's action. 'What magnificent surgery!' February was a chaotic sharing of individually discovered freedoms, October a single marvellously disciplined act, with no mention of how the recipients feel about it.

The alien rightness of the October act continues for Yurii even when leather-jacketed men 'of iron will' enter all places of work and residence and deal mercilessly with 'bourgeois' resisters. As is the case in several other historical–political contexts, the description of these men comes over as Pasternak's own, rather than as Yurii's or any intermediate narrator's. The way two fairly different things are said about them in a single sentence – they are 'armed with revolvers and with the means of terrorising' and they 'rarely shaved and still more rarely slept' – shows a still mixed attitude to them: revulsion from the cruelty, but at least some attraction to the single-minded devotion. Yurii is at one with his author here. Other doctors resign from their jobs, but he stays on and declares to all who ask that, yes, he is indeed serving 'them', and that he respects the new regime which imposes suffering on him and his family. Eventually, though, he is persuaded to leave cold, starving, hostile Moscow and travel to cold, starving, unknown but not yet hostile Varykino.

The journey there, described in Part 7, is a journey through changing weathers, from the late heavy snowfall as the train departs in April to the heat of early summer at the family's arrival perhaps a month later. On the way, the train (which must be moving unbelievably slowly) is held up for three days by snowdrifts, and as they near their destination the spring thaw comes at last with a great flowing of water, at which some of the forced-labour conscripts escape from the train. So much fine description of earth and sky under dynamically altering weathers and of feelings responding to them makes Part 7 seem an expansion of the observation, in the previous part, on the effect of the thunder: 'like electrical elements, the component parts of existence became palpable'.

But political matters return in the conversations with fellow-passengers. Yurii makes several impatient or dejected-sounding remarks, and seems to have lost his former hopefulness. To Kostoyed, the 'co-operativist' who later turns up as a Bolshevik, he says 'Why should I know everything and put myself out? The times don't consider me . . . let me too ignore the facts.' To another man of complex conviction, Samdevyatov, he says: 'This isn't life, it's something unprecedented, a phantasmagoria' and declares he no longer expects any good from violence (does that mean he would no longer use the 'surgery' metaphor?), but thinks people should be attracted to good by good; then abruptly, helplessly, he closes the conversation. It is not that Yurii lacks views or shrinks from explaining his position, but he cannot communicate with men whose heads are full of theory and power. While he distraughtly disagrees with Kostoyed and Samdevyatov, he calmly agrees with Alexander Gromeko who says: 'This philosophy is alien to me. This regime is against us. They didn't ask my consent for this rupture. But they have trusted me, and my actions, even if done under compulsion, do bind me.'

There is plenty of evidence that Yurii is no opponent of socialism, even though he has belonged to the privileged part of society. In 1917 and 1918 he feels it is right that his excess property be taken away and that he share his apartment with others; he cannot enjoy the good food chance offers his family when others are deprived of it; he notes how 'personalities' fade into nonentities the moment their 'right to idleness' is withdrawn and he clearly sympathises with his father-in-law who says he would not have his family's factories back even as a gift: 'the history of property in Russia is ended'. Then in 1920 or so we find him telling Liverii that he approves of the Bolsheviks' plans for moral and educational reform. It is not these things that distress him. Like so many thinking people of his time, he is ready, eager to become part of the new society and to work for it. What distresses him is that those who, in the heat of action, showed such vitality and originality, subsequently cannot give up the rhetoric of Revolution, their 'shrill textbook enthusiasms' (the translators have done well with this phrase), but go on and on posting up slogans and provoking hatred, thus stupefying, instead of liberating, society. For it turns out that 'the turmoil of changing and rearranging things is their only native element' and 'worlds in construction, periods of transition, are, for them, ends in themselves'. Yurii here expresses the views of very many people who lived through the Revolution and its aftermath. But there is something peculiar to him and his uncle, something very Pasternakian, in the description of the Bolshevik revolutionaries as 'untalented'. Vedenyapin used this word of the ancient Romans: they lacked the 'talent' for living. Presumably, had the Bolsheviks had 'talent', they would, once the main social-political change was brought about, have begun talking of growth rather than force, and of love rather than battle. To Pasternak – to Yurii – their continued obsession with terminology and postponement of feeling are signs of untalentedness. In Vedenyapin's terms, they are back in the 'Roman' age, or even back in 'pre-history': splendid, impersonal, cruel and – homeless.

Later, Yurii is embarrassed by the enthusiasm he felt

during the year of the Revolution, as what he then took for genius turns out to be the 'genius for self-limitation'. All the same, and although he is increasingly ill-treated and threatened by those in power, he goes on giving his assent to the regime, never regretting the Revolution or working against what it has led to. As far as he is concerned, it is a fact and it is Russia.

Yurii's criticisms are not put forward with great force. He either mutters and blurts them to opponents, or else expresses them fairly reflectively as part of a lovers' dialogue or a family conversation. He does not pronounce speeches or vigorously take sides; he does not sum things up. This humane negativity of his is shown in concentrated form in the section about the battle between Reds and Whites which he gets involved in while living with the Reds.

This section is the one the *Novyi mir* editors took most exception to. It could be read as a study in indecisiveness — or, in decisively not taking sides, in rising above dichotomies and enmities. Doctors should not fight, but our doctor feels he must join in just because he is there, so he picks up a rifle and begins firing it. At the same time he negates his action by aiming solely at a tree. (Irene Masing-Delic, in *Russian Review*, July 1981, has compellingly argued that he is firing at death itself, symbolised by the dead tree.) Yurii deeply sympathises with the Whites, who resemble the people he grew up with, but is now bound by fate and new loyalties to the Reds. He avoids supporting either side, and when he inadvertently 'kills' a man, he then saves the man's life and helps him escape. Thus in circumstances of the most urgent alignments imaginable he exemplifies the greatest possible non-alignment. His attitude is supported by his discovering, after the fighting, the very same prayer for divine protection in the pockets of two fallen men, an illiterate Red and an educated White.

The scene could remind us of how the civilian Pierre Bezukhov wanders on the battle-field at Borodino, in *War and Peace*, and seizes hold of an enemy soldier just as the latter seizes him, so that neither knows who is the captor and who the captured; or of Nikolai Rostov, in another battle in that book, looking into the French lad's eyes as he takes him prisoner. But in *War and Peace* these incidents are parts of long detailed accounts of what battles are really like and they also tell us a good deal about the heroes' characters. Pasternak is not interested in battles as such (for realistic description this section is one of the worst) and nothing new is conveyed about Yurii's character. The moral point (people are people on both sides) is baldly made. But there would seem to be another point, to be summarised perhaps like this: poetry belongs among life-giving likenesses, not among deathly disparities. The motif of the same poetic text being shared by very different kinds of people will occur again when Yurii overhears the chanting of the 'sorceress' Kubarikha; here untaught and cultured, gipsy and scholar, are inspired by the same ancient words. The poet flourishes in situations of complex interconnection and kinship, however distant, but when he finds himself in the midst of starkly oppositional thinking he is like a doctor on a battlefield.

Strelnikov and others

So far in this chapter I have been discussing Yurii Zhivago's relation to the Revolution and to revolutionaries. His relationship with the revolutionary Strelnikov belongs in another category. This is a confrontation of opposite 'ways of sensing the world' in two men who at some level are deeply bound together. It is telling that Strelnikov is not a member of any party, thus also in his own way not a side-taker, and significant too that he alone of all the other characters echoes Zhivago's preoccupation with the Book of Revelation — again in his own way, dwelling only on the destructive aspect of it: 'These are times of the Last Judgment, my dear sir', he tells Zhivago, 'creatures from the Apocalypse with swords, and winged beasts.'

When he first enters the novel as Strelnikov, at the end of Part 7, he comes as a contrast both to the vagueness of Yurii's meandering over the railway lines and to the homeliness of his own environment — at any rate as Yurii experiences the latter. Waiting to be interrogated in Strelnikov's headquarters — another train (Antipov–Strelnikov has a multitude of symbolic connections with railways) — Yurii is reassured to see people engaged in the homely business of mending a typewriter and then infuriated to see a young prisoner ramming his school-cap back onto his wounded head (uniforms should be thrown away, not clung to). Then suddenly Strelnikov 'entered with long, vigorous strides and stood in the centre of the room'.

Instantly, Yurii recognises in him a 'finished manifestation of the will'. But why is he so astonished that he has never before encountered a man 'of such definiteness'? Why should he expect to have encountered one? Presumably because this man is so profoundly his opposite that a psychic bond exists between them; each is the other's 'other', representing that way of being which the other person's way excludes and therefore darkly calls to mind and expects to meet. Here are decision and indecision, the outlined and the hazy, self-projection and self-effacement, violent activity and gentle creativity. It is a fascinating development of the Lemokh–Seryozha confrontation in 'A Tale', where the 'dry, definite and very rapid person' drove away all the poet's gaiety simply by walking into the room and, more, 'devalued him from head to foot'. For Strelnikov, who is in a position not merely to destroy this poet's self-confidence but to have him executed without trial, does not manage to devalue a hair on his head. To Strelnikov's threateningly provisional dismissal Yurii makes a reply which could be compared to the way the young nobleman Grinyov, in Pushkin's *The Captain's Daughter*, quietly stands up to the peasants' leader, Pugachov, at a risk of immediate hanging, and makes it clear that their opposition is larger than a political one:

I know everything you think about me. From your own point of view you are completely right. But the dispute into which you wish to draw me is one I have been mentally conducting all my life with an imaginary accuser, and it must be expected that I have had time to come to some sort of conclusion. This can't be told in a couple of words. Allow me to go away without explanations if I am really free, and if not − do what you like with me. There is nothing about which I have to justify myself to you. (7:31)

Among the notes which Pasternak made while writing *Doctor Zhivago* (which were made available to me by E. B. Pasternak in Moscow) is a paragraph which he must have intended at one stage to include as description of Yurii:

How he had always loved these people of conviction and deed, these fanatics of revolution and religion, how he had bowed to them! With what shame he had been covered, how unmasculine and worthless he had always seemed to himself before them! And how he had never, never set himself the aim of becoming like them or following them. His work at himself went in quite another direction.

The most remarkable points here are the word 'loved' and the attained confidence of being safely different. One might perhaps talk, in C. G. Jung's vocabulary, of Strelnikov as Zhivago's 'shadow'. The shadow is that part of oneself that one might have developed but has rejected and kept at bay, fearing its powers. There is a hint in their names: the 'anti' in Antipov need not imply 'against', but 'antipode', the other side of the coin; and *strel*, from words for 'arrow' and 'shoot', though it could suggest 'deadly', the opposite of *zhiv*: 'living' or 'lively', could also suggest the straight-to-the-point action of an arrow, as opposed to an undirected and wandering kind of living. So long as it is feared, the 'shadow' is dangerous. Once recognised and accepted, it becomes a part of one's own strength. This view seems supported by the description of Strelnikov as having, in Yurii's eyes, 'a natural, unstrained giftedness and a sense of being at home and in control in every possible earthly situation', for nearly all of this could apply to Yurii himself and shows how much the two characters have in common: a similar naturalness, an equal stature in their relation to the natural. What doesn't apply to him is the phrase 'in control' (literally 'in the saddle'), and this contains the whole of his 'otherness'.

The idea of the shadow is further supported by the fact that Strelnikov remains an enigma. He is essentially that which Zhivago cannot fully know, just as *he* cannot know Zhivago. So he cannot be summed up, is therefore not a 'type' and 'if a person is not a type, it means he has a grain of immortality'. At these words, Zhivago's, we may remember Vedenyapin saying 'immortality is another word for life'. Continually, the author makes us expect to find Strelnikov summed up as a typical revolutionary fanatic, and labelled once and for all, as he begins to be in such phrases as 'lacking the unprincipled heart' or 'sheer principle, the personification of an idea'. Yet every labelling of him is unfastened by an acknowledgment of his originality. His fanaticism, says the author, is 'not copied from anyone else, but prepared by his whole life and not random' and Lara, who calls him a personification, also sees in him 'the complete absence of pose'. All the long conversations between the lovers, in Yuryatin and Varykino, converge towards the enigma of this man. They are both drawn to him, even while sensing his harsh otherness, his different fatality. At one point Lara calls him, all in one breath: handsome, honest, resolute, manly . . . abstract, colourless, embodiment of an idea . . . marked with a sign and doomed. And while he clearly conforms to a kind of maleness, it is just as clear that he is not one of those she sums up as 'resourceful, self-assured, imperious men', so useful in practical matters but so repulsive in matters of feeling.

Mimicry is an important motif in *Doctor Zhivago*. There are two sorts. One is that which happens naturally. This occurs when Yurii, as doctor in Moscow, gazes through his office window at a falling leaf that seems to mimic a bird (as the crow mimicked a branch in his childhood fairyland); or when, in the forest, he disappears into the leaves he is lying on, meditating the while on Darwin and a self-camouflaging butterfly; or when the 'angelic' Vasya, the boy the Zhivagos meet on their long train journey, involuntarily reflects in his face all the features of a story someone is telling. The other kind is imitation of other people, the fitting of oneself into ready-made social moulds. Lara feels the risk of this 'demon of imitation' when Komarovsky seduces her – she might, she thinks, start acting the part of the Seduced Girl; on a later occasion, she observes that people getting drunk at parties tend to act the part of People Getting Drunk at Parties;

Gordon and Dudorov became examples of such imitative acting.

But what of Strelnikov? He is explicitly associated with mimicry: as a boy, he has the widow Tiverzina in fits of laughter with his talent for mimicking various acquaintances. But he is also explicitly associated with radical change of character. After Lara's confession on their wedding night he gets up 'a different person, almost surprised he still had the same name'. Just how he was changed we do not know: permanently hurt, or made more tolerant, or what? Only the fact of change as such is mentioned. Some motives are given for his decision to go to war, but once more the stress is on the sheer change: Lara says, 'I don't recognise you. Has another person been substituted for you?' Galiullin (someone who has known him from childhood and is now an army officer), meeting him at the battle-front, not only finds him an already changed man but, 'as if in the depth of a window', sees in him 'some other person' (literally 'a second someone' – mistranslated as 'some*thing*'). Next thing we know, he has become the second person, Strelnikov, paradoxically enough an incarnation of definiteness. Is this then some sort of imitation, in the bad sense? As his new self answers so well the requirements of the age, we could suppose he is copying a type. But the author will not confirm this supposition. Like the early Mayakovsky in real life, Strelnikov is not to be summarised, is always astonishing. He acts, but he has invented his own act. How, remains the mystery.

It is not solved when he turns up in Varykino after Lara has gone and he meets Zhivago again. Their conversation at once rehearses the enigma each man is to the other and brings them to a point of union as they recognise that both set out on adult life from love of the same girl at the same age in a spirit of compassion and admiration. Then the two are linked further in an image after Strelnikov's suicide: rowanberries. Earlier, these led Yurii out of captivity and now they are what Strelnikov's blood drops resemble. What for the one signifies life, for the other signifies death.

Yurii's disappearance into obscure regions of battle and turmoil, after the kidnap at the end of Part 9, is paralleled by
his disappearance from the novel for the whole of Part 10.
Instead of following him in his adventures, we are taken into
the life of a small Siberian town (called Krestovozdvizhensk:
the raising of the cross) and especially into the mind of one
Galuzina, a grocer's wife, who affords a crossing-point for
many of the novel's facts, fates and images. She has another
function too: she is the first of three characters, all female,
whom Yurii does not meet but who reflect aspects of him. All
appear only once, but briefly hold our entire attention.

Galuzina expresses in developed and particularised form
the nostalgic regret for the past which is one part of Yurii's
feeling about the times (another part is enthusiasm for the
future). In the first half of Part 10 she reminisces about small-
town life in Russia before the Revolution, settled and pro-
spering, full of the narrow but happy concerns of her
girlhood, her father's grocery store, the local eccentrics — all
of it gone for ever. Nostalgia is accompanied by physical
pains; Galuzina is in need of healing.

Kubarikha, an ageless woman in a soldier's greatcoat and
with passionate eyes, is the second of these female parallels
to Yurii. A contrast to Galuzina, she is unsettled, un-
prosperous, a vagrant and camp-follower of the partisans.
She is, like him, a healer — of cows' ulcers — and, like him,
a poet — improviser of folksong and of a spell-binding mixture of legend, chronicle and popular sayings. She is his link
with folk-wisdom and the deep past and she inspires him with
vision and the urge to escape.

The third figure is Sima Tuntseva, an intellectual. Back in
Yuryatin, Yurii overhears Sima (as he overheard Kubarikha)
expounding her thoughts about the Bible. A fundamental
shift has taken place in the notion of the miraculous. While
the Old Testament saw miracle in multitudinous events like a
whole nation crossing over a sea-bed with the sea held back
by divine intervention, the New Testament sees it in the quiet
birth of a provincial baby. The precious and vulnerable
change from thinking in terms of nations and races to

thinking in terms of persons, from worship of the heroic to worship of the humble, is a repeated theme in *Doctor Zhivago*.

While these three women represent aspects of Yurii — his love of continuity and home, his poetry and healing, his intense wonder at ordinary existence — the three women he falls in love with appear to represent femininity as such. That they come, before the Revolution, from different social backgrounds (large property owners, struggling business folk, servant class) throws into prominence what they have in common: strong emotion and certain womanly abilities. All are in some measure associated with water, which symbolises life, liberation and renewal. With Tonya, Yurii travels over fields that have become an ocean of thawed snow. Lara is connected with a number of water images — thunderstorms, pouring rain, water from a well. The relationship with Marina, whose name means 'sea-scape', starts with his fetching several buckets of much-needed water from her home. With its dominant theme of love for women, the positive value of the element associated with them and the reflection of Yurii's own strengths in three women, rather than in other men, *Doctor Zhivago* seems altogether a more woman-oriented than masculine novel. The author acknowledges, admires and is drawn to masculinity, but is never quite identified with it, looking at it as if across a space.

Moreover, the men come in for more criticism than the women. Two men who seem present in the novel mainly in order to be criticised are the two we meet in Part 1 and then for long periods lose sight of: Misha Gordon and Nika Dudorov. Except when Gordon shares Yurii's thoughts during the war in Part 3, he and Dudorov are presented through much of the book by a series of short, adjectival summings-up, which do not add up to coherent or developing characters. These two are 'effaced': not by being left undescribed, like Tonya, or by being extended into suprapersonal significance, like Lara, but by having fixed characteristics ascribed to them which fail to cohere. Thus Dudorov in 1905 appears to Vedenyapin as a desperate revolutionary schoolboy, and to Lara as 'straightforward, taciturn and proud'; in 1917 he appears to Misha as ludicrously absent-minded, eccentric, neurotic, while the author tells us he has changed from being extremely unstable to being a concentrated scholar who talks in a monotonous nasal voice. Towards the end of the book he virtually merges with Gordon and they begin to be mentioned only as a pair, somewhat like Shakespeare's Rosencrantz and Guildenstern, a parallel which may have been in Pasternak's mind since Zhivago's first poem suggests a connection with *Hamlet*. Gordon, too, consists of a chain of not incompatible and yet scarcely connected impressions, made mostly on other characters but sometimes, disconcertingly, on the author.

Perhaps the point is that every observer notes different features and deduces the existence of a somewhat different person. So Gordon's change from gloomy and inarticulate to cuttingly witty only seems unlikely because the qualities, observed by different people, are stated so starkly, without explanatory links. Or perhaps the two exemplify from the beginning what they turn out, in the end, to have become: men who change with changing circumstances, always assimilating to some external model, never being themselves – mimics in the bad sense. For they are finally seen through Yurii's eyes alone and judged as second-rate minds, philistines and conformists: men who, having been imprisoned, now idealise lack of freedom.

There are some sentences in Part 15 in which Pasternak's own anger and distress at Soviet intellectual conditions certainly break through, to the detriment of verisimilitude. 'It was precisely the stereotype quality in what Dudorov was saying and feeling that Gordon found particularly touching. The textbook orthodoxy of their sentiments he took for their human universality.' Yurii judges them, but not (as some readers have thought he does) from any high and mighty position. Hating the way they talk, he wishes he could say to them 'the only good thing about you is that you live at the same time as I do' but instead of saying it he simply walks away from them, helplessly coughing, beginning to suffocate.

And yet it is Gordon and Dudorov who are found at the

very end reading Zhivago's works with understanding, and feeling – along with the author – the spirit of the future. Have they been influenced by their poet-friend after all? Or do their fleeting individual characteristics finally dissolve into something all-encompassing and all-redeeming? Or are they, here and previously, just any two men, with no necessary names, vehicles of posterity and of poetry's survival?

Coincidences

While 'effacing' psychology, Pasternak sharply delineates certain wider aspects of life and among these are the 'crossings of fate' mentioned in the poem 'Winter Night': the chance criss-crossings of biographical paths. Zhivago's life is filled with such crossings. Some lead to important relationships, others seem insignificant. It is by chance that Lara is a nurse in the ward he is taken to when wounded, and fate or chance twice brings Strelnikov into his life. And he repeatedly comes across people he has heard of or come across before: Pelageya, whom he met on the train journey; Pamfil Palykh who turns out to be the murderer of Gintz; Vasya and many others.

A great deal has been written about the coincidences in *Doctor Zhivago*, some critics saying they are too many and too prominent, others saying there are only as many as usually do occur in our lives, and yet others that their meaning is that all lives are joined in a great pattern of destiny. Lara once mentions destiny in this sense (13:12). But it is more interesting, I think, to note that the author often foregrounds coincidences which are not at all surprising: that is, not what we would usually call a 'coincidence' at all. One example may stand for many.

In a forest-glade during World War I, Yurii, Lara, Galiullin and others, including a badly wounded and dying man who happens to be Galiullin's father, are all by chance together. The author draws attention to this with a paragraph that on rapid reading could seem to say: 'look how astonishing: they all knew one another before!' This is what it does say, however:

The mutilated man who had died was the private in the reserve Gimazetdin, the officer shouting in the forest was his son, Lieutenant Galliullin, the nurse was Lara, the witnesses were Gordon and Zhivago. All of them were together, all side by side, and some did not recognise one another, others had never known one another, and some things remained forever unconfirmed, others began waiting for other occasions, another encounter, to be revealed.   (4:10)

'Others had never known one another' – what kind of coincidence (in the usual sense) can this be? Why bother to point out that some people met who had not met before? And how should we read the long piece about what the future will, or will not, confirm or reveal? The answer must be that every meeting is astonishing and any configuration of people may be seen as a nodal point between past and future. Everything that has happened or is to happen is part of one whole thing. Life's patterns are partly observable, partly hidden and the hidden parts lead off into linkages elsewhere, eventually into something conceived as a totality: that coherence of all lives which in Part 1 the author described with such warmth.

Pasternak wrote in *A Safe Conduct* of how 'poetry was born' in his life: not from inner processes, and not from any one incident or accumulation of incidents, but from the 'differences in speed' among the many things that happened, by chance, to be taking place at the same moment; from their 'interruptions' of one another and irregularities of movement, some lagging far behind, others rushing ahead. This is one of the thoughts, expressed rather compactly, even obscurely, in the earlier work, which are repeated in the novel in loosened, simplified form. At the book's opening Yurii's father's suicide takes place, by coincidence, near the house Yurii is staying in, and in a cluster of other potential coincidences. Then near the end of the book Yurii's own death is a paradigm of coincidence and of meditation upon it.

It is while preoccupied with the thought of how several lives may run parallel and close together yet move at different speeds that Yurii has a heart-attack and stumbles out of the tram to fall dead at the roadside. There is no word of lament or suggestion of loss. Quite the contrary is indicated. For all the while a greyhaired old lady who, we are informed, is none other than Mademoiselle Fleury — Yurii's acquaintance from long ago in Melyuzeev, who has dropped completely out of his life and out of the novel up till now — has been walking along the pavement, making a totally unnoticed counterpoint of movements with the tram, catching up, overtaking, getting left behind. He does not see her. She does not recognise him. It is clear they could just as well be two people who have *not* met before — it 'makes no difference', it would still be as amazing. After his collapse she walks on, busy with her own thoughts and cares, 'wholly unaware that she had overtaken Zhivago and survived him'.

Life continues, its patterns are not broken. To emphasise that this crossing of fates is a happy occasion, the author tells us that the old lady is wearing lilac, a colour once amply associated with happiness (in Galuzina's meditations); her name, moreover, betokens flowers, and the flowers surrounding Yurii's coffin (this is a page later) are said 'perhaps to contain the mysteries of transformation'.

Coincidence gathers thick and fast as Yurii's body is laid out in the very room where Pasha (Strelnikov) once lived, and as Lara chances to return from the far east that very day and turn up in that room. There is nothing surreal or symbolistic about it, but the coffin scene becomes a lyrical collocation of life-affirming motifs, culminating in Lara's grieving words, in which lament is overcome by re-assertion of the belief in a universal coherence and sharing.

Chapter 6

Style and method; Errors and contiguities; Problems of translation

A comparison of the style of *Doctor Zhivago* with that of *A Safe Conduct* will show how Pasternak changed between 1930 and 1950, as he worked towards a 'restrained, unpretentious style'. In *A Safe Conduct* he describes a train journey he made at night over the Swiss Alps, waking for short moments to marvel at where he was:

The dark was totally opaque, but echoes filled it with a rotund sculpture of sounds. Chasms conversed unashamedly loudly, like old gossips pulling the earth to bits in their talk. Everywhere streams were rumouring and prattling and filtering through. It was easy to guess how they were hung out all over the steeps and were let down into the valley like twisted threads. While, from above, vertically overhanging boulders leapt down onto the train, settled themselves on the carriage roofs and, with shouts to each other and dangling their feet, enjoyed a free ride.

But sleep overcame me and I kept falling into an impermissible slumber on the threshold of the snows, under the blind white Oedipal eyes of the Alps, on the peak of the demonic perfection of the planet.(Quoted from *Pasternak on Art and Creativity*, page 111)

A passage in *Doctor Zhivago* which is also about sleeping at night in a train and briefly waking to marvel at the surroundings dwells similarly on sensations of height and expanse, and is similarly about falling water, though here not sound but silence is evoked:

Yurii Andreevich awoke early in the night from a confused feeling of happiness that filled him to overflowing and was so strong that it woke him. The train was standing at some nocturnal halt. Around the station gathered the glassy dusk of a white night. This bright darkness was suffused with something subtle and powerful. It betokened the breadth and openness of the place and hinted that the station stood on a height with a wide free range of vision.

Along the platform inaudibly stepping shadows moved past the carriage, conversing quietly. Yurii Andreevich was touched by this as well. In the carefulness of the footsteps and the voices he sensed respect for the night hour and a care for those sleeping in the train — the way it could have been in the old days, before the war.

The doctor was mistaken. On the platform people were making a racket and stamping their boots, like everywhere else. But there was a waterfall in the neighbourhood. It was pushing back the borders of the white night with an atmosphere of freshness and freedom. It was instilling the feeling of happiness in the doctor in his sleep. The incessant, never-stopping noise of its watery avalanche dominated all other sounds in the station and created the illusion of silence.

Not guessing its presence, but lulled by the mysterious resilience of the air in that place, the doctor again fell fast asleep.   (7:21)

The first passage is full of invention and discovery. It makes exuberant use of anthropomorphism (chasms conversed . . . boulders leapt and shouted) and of synaesthesia (a rotund sculpture of sounds . . . prattling and filtering) — all in the interest of finding exact correlates for new strong perceptions. The second insists far less on verbal originality. The images are impressive but not astonishing — 'glassy dusk' and 'watery avalanche' are phrases we could all perhaps imagine ourselves saying if we were there. In the earlier piece joy, excitement and delight are implicit, not named. In the latter, a feeling of happiness is mentioned twice, explicit and not to be overlooked, as are other sensations or feelings: respect, freshness, freedom. In the *Safe Conduct* piece the sensation of height and the detailed falling of water are direct sources of pleasure; in the *Zhivago* piece, the pleasure, though ultimately due to the falling water, has also a moral content: the waterfall causes a grateful impression of people being considerate to one another. The idea of a community based on kindness and courtesy arises in the second paragraph here. The *Safe Conduct* piece appeals to something more aesthetic and difficult: 'the demonic perfection of the planet'. Perfection here means rare physical beauty, sheer height, sheer verticality, a miracle of nature. But in the *Zhivago* piece even the words describing the natural environs have a moral sound to them: 'breadth and openness . . . a wide free range of vision', and nature is invoked for a philosophical message, perhaps that everything is united, or can be, in one element; everything can undergo transformation at once.

The second excerpt differs also from the first in its tendency to be explanatory. 'The doctor supposed one thing to be the case, but really something else was, namely . . .' – this is its rhetorical shape. A tone of explanation is there from the beginning, even to the point of tautology: he 'woke . . . from a feeling that was so strong that it woke him'. In *Doctor Zhivago* Pasternak very much wants to be understood. Everything is spelled out. Often metaphors are analysed on the spot, almost apologised for. Whereas in *A Safe Conduct* he was able to write that life's laconicism 'crossed the road and took me by the hand', in *Zhivago* he will not write 'the storm noticed Yura' but instead 'it was possible to imagine that the storm had noticed . . .' (1:2). Our quoted excerpt, too, says in various ways: 'it was possible to imagine' that the station stood on a height, that there was silence, that people were respectful.

In describing a single enormous force affecting and suffusing every aspect of the scene, the waterfall passage is typical of the numerous descriptions in the novel which show things changing under the influence of the wind, a storm, a burst of light, a heavy darkness or a roar of noise. Here is an example:

Over the town, as if crazy, clouds were racing as though running away from pursuit. Their tatters were flying past so low that they almost caught onto the trees that were leaning in the same direction, so it seemed as if the sky were being swept with them as with bending besoms.
(5:9)

The act of comparison is self-consciously set out – 'it seemed as if' – but does not hold up the impression of speed and change under the force of the wind and the intense interaction of things at their edges or borders.

Pasternak's love of changing weathers is insatiable. Even after acknowledging that a certain weather would seem 'awful' to most people, he will go on to describe it with evident ecstasy.

The weather was the most awful that could be imagined. Low over the earth a sharp fitful wind carried torn shreds of storm-clouds black as flakes of soot. Then suddenly snow was starting to pour out of them, in the convulsive haste of some white lunacy. Within a moment the distance was being veiled in a white cerement and the earth covered in a white shroud. Next minute the shroud was burning up, melting to nothing. Now there came forth a coal-black earth, and a black sky streaming with the distant slanting swellings of spent downpours. The earth was taking in no more water. In moments of brightening, the clouds would part as if someone up above were airing the sky by opening windows which gave off a glassy cold whiteness. And from the earth, the standing water not absorbed by the soil answered with its similar flung-open windows of puddles and lakes, full of the same shining.   (12:5)

The submission of everything at once to the action of a single force, the speed of change, the interweaving of opposites (black and white), the combining of earth with sky, the household imagery (brooms in the last example, airing the sky by opening windows here), the idea of saturation, and above all the final comparison to windows – all are highly characteristic signs of the delight which fills the novel and which is once referred to as a force on its own account. Looking out of the window in Melyuzeev, Zhivago hears a woman soothing a newly bought cow (a herald of Kubarikha?) and senses how 'delight in life . . . moved in a broad wave, at random over the earth and town, across walls and fences, through timber and body, and made everything in its path begin to tremble' (5:6).

Errors and contiguities

The description of the waterfall also provides an example of a feature of the novel we have not mentioned hitherto. It is something strangely easy to miss, yet – once noticed – very conspicuous. 'The doctor was mistaken': everything hinges on his mistake. Perceptual or interpretational mistakes made by characters crop up in *Doctor Zhivago* with a frequency that is far from haphazard. They should perhaps be called errors rather than mistakes, as they are often a kind of wandering from the point, and 'integral errors' since they are not supplanted by their correction.

Often an account is given of a wrong assumption about something in advance of the true account of it, or a misperception precedes the accurate perception. At the very start of the book, in its second paragraph, the answer given to those who assume that a Zhivago funeral means Mr Zhivago's is 'No, not his. Hers.' The anonymous bystander has made a wrong assumption. This is followed by another example of unnamed persons making a wrong assumption: they think the boy is about to make a speech; and then by another: he looks as if he is going to raise his head and howl like a wolf cub − instead he bows his head and sobs. So in the opening section a correct version of something is introduced, three times, through an incorrect one.

Subsequently, named persons make wrong assumptions. Tiverzin thinks he alone started the railwaymen's strike. Lara thinks she is a burden to the Kologrivovs. Another kind of error is Anna Gromeko's who, when the wardrobe falls on her, mistakenly nicknames it 'Askold's grave', meaning to say 'Oleg's horse' (in the story Prince Oleg's death is caused by his horse). At the Christmas party, Lara's wrong assumption that Komarovsky is seducing yet another girl is set forth at considerable length, and it is followed by Yurii wrongly thinking she is being rough-handled when she collapses after firing the gun and has to be helped along. Similarly, in the forest scene in the war, Lara wrongly supposes that the men helping the badly wounded soldier are about to do him some harm. 'Have you gone mad?' she cries, and again there are several paragraphs about the error, which is not cleared up. This episode echoes an earlier one where Yurii, rushing towards his wife who has just given birth, is stopped by the gynaecologist who assumes he is going to do some harm and says 'have you gone mad?' There are many more such errors, often narrated unemphatically, yet conspicuous by being there at all. Why does the story move, in part, through them? When he does see his wife in the hospital, Yurii mistakes the height of her bed, thinking it as high as a stand-up writing-desk. When a thief breaks into her flat after the farewell party, Lara at first takes him for Pasha. At the end of Part 9 comes a particularly conspicuous example of mistaken assumption. Yurii, in the midst of his indecision, riding first home to Tonya then back to Lara, is stopped in the forest by three men on horseback and kidnapped. He supposes that Liverii, the partisan leader he has heard so much of, will be one of the three, and the reader too supposes Part 9 is about to culminate in the introduction of Liverii. But to his question comes the reply 'No, I'm Kamennodvorskii.' That is, 'I'm someone else': pure anti-climax. The entire part ends with this avoidance of a dramatic confrontation, its replacement by an error. Reality turns out to be just to one side of where we are all looking.

The error made by Anna Gromeko is given this commentary: 'As a woman of unsystematic reading she confused contiguous concepts.' It calls to mind the essay in which Roman Jakobson describes Pasternak as a metonymical writer, distinguishing him from the metaphorical Mayakovsky, and in which he outlines two distinct literary modes related to the two poetic devices. (See Donald Davie and Angela Livingstone, *Pasternak*, 1969.) The metaphorical mode is that in which objects and topics are connected by their similarity, the metonymic that in which they are connected by proximity or contiguity: they are next to each other, touch each other, border with each other. Not that Pasternak lacks metaphor, but metonymy, says Jakobson, is the more characteristic of him. He goes on to claim that in Pasternak's work 'the hero's activity eludes our perception; action is replaced by topography'. Perhaps 'topography' can be translated as the writing of places, or writing that implies people by describing places. Jakobson's essay is dated 1935 but this notion is very applicable to *Doctor Zhivago*, in which celebration of existence is so often expressed as celebration of place. Topography in this sense has characterised Pasternak's writing from the beginning: in *My Sister Life* (1917) one poem defines the soul as something which knows that it is 'here' (*zdes'*): and in another, defining creativity, the assertion that 'gardens, ponds and fences, and the whole universe' consist solely of human passion could well be reversed to say that feeling is nothing if only inward but is everything when projected into our surroundings — into places with their boundaries, or place altogether, the universe as a place. For Pasternak, love of place is love of being.

The notion of metonymy can be applied to what I have been calling integral errors. If mistakes are thought of as related to accurate versions by a kind of spatial proximity (the confusing of 'contiguous concepts'), then to pay so much attention to the mistakes people make, as Pasternak does, must suggest something like the filling out of a landscape, with guesswork and fallible impression contributing as much as accurate perception to a true topography of the world.

Very often, too, Pasternak describes things as resembling or coming to resemble one another simply by being in the same place, being next to one another. The innocence of the young men fighting in the streets in 1905 is described as spreading to everything around them. The ruined wood of a train carriage resembles not only the nearby forest and the birch fungus there, but the clouds which are part of the same visual scene. The embarrassment of the Zhivagos arriving in Varykino to find their hosts don't want them spreads to horses, gnats and everything else in the vicinity. At the street celebrations in Part 10 all noticeable objects are pink, blue or white. There are some sentences in the novel in which Pasternak seems almost to make a declaration of his metonymic method. He will say, for instance: 'Something similar was happening in the moral world and the physical, near and far off, on the earth and in the air.' Continually he stresses how things in adjoining places or categories appear alike.

The frequency of descriptions of windows in *Doctor Zhivago* (one critic has counted 220) is a sign of this same preoccupation. While for Lara windows are channels of energy — she decides to leave home whilst she sits by the open classroom window with a storm wind coming in, and water bursts in through the window to her former Melyuzeev room — in relation to Yurii and Vedenyapin windows demonstrate that the same light or energy or mood exists outside as well as inside. The contiguous areas are united:

A column of cooled air, one and the same both outdoors and within the dwelling, made him akin to the passers-by in the evening street, to the moods in the town, to the life in the world. (13:4)

Metonymy, or 'topography' in Jakobson's sense, often operates in accounts of how people perceive each other. The young Pasha, in love with Lara, feels towards her as if she were 'some kind of birch-grove at holiday time with pure grass and clouds': as if she were a place. In the Yuryatin library, watching the town's inhabitants come in, Yurii has the sensation 'as if into the reading-room were flowing not people coming in to read, but the houses and streets in which they lived': as if they were places. It seems the most essential thing about anyone is his or her local surroundings. This has nothing to do with the pathetic fallacy, the idea that human emotion is reflected in the world around. That idea points inward: the raging storm speaks of the rage in my heart. Nor has it to do with reading someone's personality from the signs of it in his surroundings. That points inward too: in *Crime and Punishment* the narrowness of Raskolnikov's room indicates and reinforces the narrowed preoccupations of his mind. Pasternak's method points outward. The flowing water of thaw and waterfall does not reflect the flight of the conscripts from the train, on the contrary, their escape copies *it*: 'they ran as the water runs'. Lying in autumn leaves in the forest, Yurii disappears into them – copies them.

Representation of people as places comes into Yurii's trance-like meditation on Kubarikha's incantations. He is so enchanted by her own and others' distortions of the legends – that is by their errings from the path of mechanical copying – that he himself distorts something she has recited about opening up women's shoulders to take out wheat, squirrels and honeycomb:

Lara's left shoulder had been half-opened. In the depth of the spiritual cavity revealed, there appeared the secrets kept by her soul. Unfamiliar cities that she had visited, alien streets, alien houses,

alien spaces, stretched out like ribbons, the unrolling skeins of
ribbons, bundles of ribbons tumbling out.   (13:7)

Straight after this section comes something like a ghastly
literal version of what is here figurative and visionary: a dying
man crawls into the partisans' camp with his right arm and
left leg chopped off and tied to his back. But before this
shock we are briefly transported into folk-tale where the
sword in the shoulder is a revelation of truth. Open a person
and you'll find places: cities unfamiliar to others, not to her,
spaces alien to others, for they are where she has been. Her
whole inner self is the outer world she has known.

   Related to this is the trance Lara falls into while standing
in the kitchen (see chapter 4). It is filled with an uncanny
aural contemplation of a hobbled horse which has strayed
into the yard beneath her window:

Over the yard a hobbled horse was moving with difficulty, in little
limping jumps. He was nobody knew whose and he had wandered
into the yard, probably by mistake. It was already completely light,
but still far from sunrise. The sleeping town, as if quite extinct, was
immersed in the grey-lilac cool of the early hour. Lara closed her
eyes. God knows to what rural remoteness and loveliness she was
carried by this distinctive incomparable iron-shod stepping of the
horse.   (4:4)

So much more attention is given to this random horse in a
random yard, this tiny moment in a town at dawn and this
fleeting thought of a far-off countryside, than is given to
Lara's relationship with the people she has just left, even
though these include her former seducer and her best friend,
that I believe we are right in finding several kinds of more
than realistic significance in it. First, it is a central example
of the virtue of erring. The horse has not merely wandered
into the yard, it has done so explicitly 'by mistake', Lara has
apparently also wandered into the kitchen by mistake, and
now all this errancy produces a dream of beauty. Secondly,
it is a central example of the presenting of people through
places, for the yard below and the evoked countryside fill
Lara's consciousness, constituting, for the moment, what she
'is', what the 'headlamps' of her consciousness light up.

Location, the experience of being in and of a particular place, the sense of being 'here', so important throughout *Doctor Zhivago*, seems an easier, expanded, God-given version of Rilke's hard-won assertion in the seventh Duino Elegy: '*Hier-sein ist herrlich.*' Being-here is splendid. Indeed, another poem by Rilke may be consciously recalled here too: the sonnet about a wandering and space-evoking hobbled horse Rilke once saw in Russia (*Sonnets to Orpheus*, I:20). Thirdly, as a landscape clearly depending on someone's perception, it illustrates a remarkable sentence in *A Safe Conduct* about 'what it is like for the visible when it begins to be seen' and the central notion there of the world changed by our feeling (see chapter 2). Finally, if we ask why it is a horse that she sees and why a hobbled one, the explanation may be that this horse represents the poet, fettered and constrained in the world of action, making mistakes, straying hither and thither and yet able to evoke, by the very stumbling of his footsteps, visions of 'rural remoteness and loveliness'. As at the Zhivagos' party, clarity and vision are right there outside the window, contrasting with the smoke and clutter of talk within.

Pasternak once wrote that, as distinct from poetry which 'seeks the melody of nature in the noise of the dictionary', prose 'seeks and finds the human being in the category of speech'. A large amount of the text of *Doctor Zhivago* is devoted to various kinds of speaking. Contrasting with pretentious chatter and pompous speech-making, as well as with the scarcely individualised talk of Yurii and those who share his voice, is another kind of talking. On the train journey, Kostoyed's peroration about the needs of the peasantry is followed by Vasya's near-verbless outburst as the train approaches his home:

Buiskoe village. Sure I know it! Our turning. From here, to our place, to the right, the right, to Veretenniki and to yours, Uncle Kharitonych, surely to the left, away from the river? Heard of the river Pelga? Well! Our river. And along the shore, the shore, to our place   (7:13) and this in turn is followed by the guard's semi-comprehensible Ukrainian. No dialogue develops, and it seems these are examples of speaking modes offered for their own sake, for their sheer diversity − as well as showing how times of social upheaval bring diverse folk together.

Everywhere, beside the lives of the main characters, are people of many different classes, occupations, levels of education, geographical origins, involved in their own affairs and talking about them, all briefly individualised through idiosyncrasies of speech. There is the servants' dispute at the Montenegro hotel, the cook Ustinya's 'bouts of unbridled spell-muttering', the broken Russian of Mademoiselle Fleury, the confused articulation of Kolya the telephonist trying to connect lines while being interrupted, the deaf-mute's outlandish diction, the strangely named peasant driver Vakkh (Bacchus) with his sing-song talk full of regional and invented oddities and oaths that fall into rhythms as if about to create proverbs, and, perhaps most important of them all, the cow-charmer's mixing of written and spoken idioms. Attention is drawn to this element in the novel when the town Zybushino is praised for its 'peculiarities of speech'. A fundamental creativity, life's 'uninterrupted self-renewal' that Yurii talks of to Liverii, is constantly at work in ordinary, everyday speech.

Words are often altered, foreign words merging into Russian-sounding ones. *Sabotage-nik* becomes *sovatazhnik* (gang-comrade), *veterinarka* (veterinary) becomes *vetre-nyanka* (wind-woman), Laiosh (a Hungarian name) becomes *layushchii* (the barker), and Galiullin (a Tatar name) becomes all sorts of things including at one point Galileyev, a fleeting reference to Galilee. In the cow-spell episode, Kubarikha invents a wonderful Russian-sounding word, *proleta*, combining *proletarii* (proletarian) with the substantival form of *bednota* (poverty, poor folk). The process of assimilation of one thing to another that we saw in the 'category-crossing' similes is thus present in individual words. Words are not fixed, but they open into each other, influenced by what is nearest, affected by what is adjacent to and contiguous with them, what meets them at their borders.

Problems of translation

The many varieties of speech are amongst the hardest tasks
for the translator. Another problem for the translator is what
to do about names. Some can be translated, for example the
names Silver Street and Silent Street (actual Moscow streets),
at the crossing of which all sorts of strange things happen to
Yurii Zhivago, and which may or may not suggest the 'silver
age' in Russian literature and its subsequent period of silence
under Stalin. But many cannot – indeed it is not customary
to translate personal names, however meaningful they are.
This means that much is lost in English. Many minor and
incidental characters have elaborately interpretable names,
such as the deaf-mute anarchist revolutionary whom Yurii
meets on the train in Part 4: Maksim Aristarkhovich
Klintsov-Pogorevshikh. *Maksim* suggests maximalism, going
to extremes; *Aristarkh* suggests severe criticism; *Klintsov* is
from *klinok*, a dagger-blade; '*Pogorevshikh*' means people
who have lost their homes in a fire. We are tacitly invited to put
these concepts together to constitute the man's significance.
But how to translate him? The major characters usually have
unremarkable, common names: Yurii, Alexander, Nikolai,
Tonya, Anna, Lara. But Komarovsky, with his name and
patronymic, Victor Ippolitovich, asks to be deciphered. A
conqueror? An unharnesser of horses (*Ippolit* – not so rare
in Russian as in English)? And *komar* – a mosquito? There
are several ways of combining these concepts, but the
translator cannot help.

The English translation of *Doctor Zhivago* available to us is
notable for a fairly high degree of accuracy. But it suffers
from the haste with which it was done. The translators
themselves have admitted not having done justice to Pasternak's style; yet at the same time they claim that the general
impression his style makes is 'fluent, natural, colloquial, con-
versational' (Manya Harari in *Encounter*, vol. 5–6, 1959).
Certainly it is far more fluent and natural than his style in the
1920s and some of it is colloquial; but much of it is not

fluent at all, much is highly poetic, and very often there is an underlying oddness, elusiveness, indirectness which the translators seem to have forcibly eliminated. All too often they substitute an expected word where Pasternak has an unexpected one, omit a phrase, drop an adjective or two, take a sentence apart and reconstruct it — all to *make* Pasternak fluent and natural.

Occasionally their decisions are understandable. Part 10 opens like this:

There were towns, villages, settlements. The town Krestovozd-vizhensk, the station Omel'chino, Pazhinsk, Tysyatskoye, the hamlet Yaglinskoye, Zvonarskaya area, the camp Vol'noye, Gurtov-shchiki, Kezhemskaya suburb, the settlement Kazeevo, the region Kuteiny garden, the village Little Ermolai

and readers may say it is just as well to have this reduced to: 'There were towns, villages and Cossak settlements.' Yet a note on their omission could have reminded us how much Pasternak loved names, and loved ringing the changes on words — here, tellingly, a series of nine different nouns for inhabited places, human environments: a pointer to his concern with 'topography'. Similarly the words 'Agatha, Pamphil's wife', are an unacknowledged abbreviation by the translators of: 'Palykh, the wife of Pamfil, Agafya Fotievna, colloquially called Fatevna' (12:7) — by which Pasternak calls our attention both to the theme of changing and evolving words and to the sheer abundance of names adhering everywhere to the minor characters. Examples of the omission of names could be greatly multiplied.

Of course many things other than names cannot be rendered in translation. A church bell (10:3) is described as emitting a 'wave of quiet dark sweet humming' and these adjectives with their repeated endings — *tikhovo, tyomnovo i sladkovo gudeniya* (the noun half-rhymes too) — themselves suggest the faint continuing hum. There is a great deal of sound-effect like this, carrying over from Pasternak's lifelong work at the craft of poetry. Something else that occasionally carries over is a habit of bringing words together into a pattern of similar consonants. Thus the Tolstoyan (in 2:10) has the surname Vyvolochnov, and *voloch* (suggesting 'dragging') is echoed in words referring to him: *volochitsya* (dragged), *voilochnaya* (made of felt), and *razoblachayas'* (disrobing). This practice of alliteration, assonance and the echoing of whole syllables plays its part in creating a style that often eludes translation.

Let us look briefly at two sentences, to illustrate both the difficulty of translating this novel and the shortcomings of the translation that we have. In 10:3, undersized apple-trees 'were miraculously (or: wonderfully, marvellously) flinging their branches from gardens across fences onto the street' (*chudesnym obrazom perekidyvali iz sadov vetki cherez zabory na ulitsu*). Max Hayward and Manya Harari diminish this to 'reached miraculously across the garden fences'. But 'reached' has none of the force of *perekidyvali*, and 'onto the street' is vitally important to Pasternak, with his passion for the explicit bridging and linking of proximate places.

The paragraph continues: 'From them, making knocking sounds at different instants from one another (or: disjointedly knocking to one another − with strong suggestion of prisoners in neighbouring cells communicating through the wall), drops were falling onto the wooden pavements. Their uncoordinated drumming (or: drum-like irregular beating) resounded through the whole town' (*S nikh, nedruzhno perestukivayas', padali kapli na derevyannye trotuary. Barabannyi raznoboi ikh razdavalsya po vsemu gorodu*). Hayward and Harari deal with the difficult phrases by omitting the first and greatly reducing the second, while twice introducing the word 'water', which Pasternak does not use: 'Drops of water dripped from them and the drumming of the water on the wooden pavements could be heard right across the town.' Again the parts which are left out, about the irregularity, intermittency, of the sounds, are of the greatest significance in the symbolism of the novel.

The quoted sentences are from the British edition of 1958, which has recently been re-issued and remains the only version of the book available in Britain. In the same year as it came out there appeared an American edition which contained

numerous changes, many of which are corrections and
stylistic improvements. For example, where Pasternak writes,
in 12:7: 'A great and powerful feeling is sometimes to be
found in the world. In it there is always an admixture of pity'
(*Inogda vstrechaetsya na svete bol'shoe i sil'noe chuvstvo. K
nemu vsegda primeshivaetsya zhalost'*), we find that the
English edition inexplicably renders this very positive statement by a double negative: 'No deep and strong feeling such
as we may come across here and there in the world is unmixed
with compassion' — in which 'here and there' is quite wrong
too and the combination of two sentences into one under-
mines the leisureliness which Pasternak is introducing at this
point. A few lines later comes the sentence 'They are jealous
of the surrounding air . . . for possession of her' (*Oni
revnuyut yeyo k okruzhayushchemu vozdukhu*), which,
neglecting the several passages in the novel outlining an un-
conventional (metonymic!) view of jealousy, the translators
gave as: 'He sees her at the mercy of the surrounding air.' In
the American (Pantheon Books) edition all this was corrected. However, although the latter is often much more
faithful, and more readable too, it introduces mistakes of its
own, and it too omits innumerable sentences and phrases. In
5:16 Pasternak writes: 'A sloping field, rising out of a hollow,
moved off into the distance in a wide mound', but the
American edition of the translation, like the British, leaves
out the phrase I have italicised, thus losing half of the movement and failing to attend to Pasternak's conception of the
world: 'A sloping field rose from a hollow to a wide mound.'
This is a tiny example, taken at random, but it is one of very
many. The American version follows the British one, too, in
not even attempting to render most of the speech rhythms so
carefully reproduced and elaborated by Pasternak. Again to
take but one instance: both editions ignore the rhythmic
repetitiousness and paratactic simplicity of Kubarikha's
incantations in 12:7.

Winter will come, the blizzard will come, to whirl a crowd of winds
in the field and twist up pillars. And I'll plunge you a knife in that
pillar of snow, in that whirl of snow, I'll drive you a knife right

into the snow, to the very hilt, and out of the snow I'll pull
it all red and bloody (*Pridet zima, poidet metelitsa v pole
vikhri tolpit', kruzhit' stolbunki. I ya tebe v tot stolb
snegovoi, v tot snegovorot nozh zaluknu, vgonyu nozh v sneg
po samyi cherenok, i ves' krasnyi v krovi iz snega vynu*).

This is ironed out into a single sentence with two unjustified
'when' clauses:

When the winter comes with blizzards and whirlwinds and
snowspouts chasing each other in the fields, I will stick a knife into
such a pillar of snow, right up to the hilt, and when I take it out of
the snow, it will be red with blood.

Pasternak's prose in the novel is not as fluent and familiar as
the translators would have us think. In turning it into easier,
quicker and thinner English, they have made it appear less
sensitive than it is, at times less naive, at times less visionary,
and altogether (as though clumsily trying to help him achieve
his 'unnoticeable style') less strange, original and interesting.

Chapter 7

The poems

Part 17 consists of 'The Poems of Yurii Zhivago'. Far from being a mere appendix, such as the English edition has made of them, the poems are integral to the book, its last, completing, chapter. So we should not stop reading when the narrative portion of the text comes to an end, reserving the poems for some later, different attention, but should read straight on from 'The book in their hands gave their feelings support and confirmation' to 'The roar's gone quiet. I've come out on the stage' which could well be the words printed in the 'book in their hands'. I do not agree with Donald Davie that the poems are needed as 'proof' that Zhivago is a poet — a novel does enough if it informs us that its hero is a writer, or portrays him at his writing-desk: we are willing to imagine his poems just as we imagine the music attributed to a fictional composer. But he is surely right to argue that *Doctor Zhivago* is 'one whole thing, intricately interlocking, in which prose supports poetry and vice versa'. This chapter will look at aspects of that interlocking.

The poems were written by Pasternak between 1946 and 1953, years in which he was working on the novel. Yet they are offered as written by Yurii Zhivago. Author and character are identified at this point. Their identification may go still further. Zhivago's aspirations with regard to writing are Pasternak's own. One of them, the wish for 'an unnoticeable style', he does, apparently, achieve, both in the poems with their relatively straightforward manner and unimpeded style, and in the 'small books' he publishes, which are said to be read with pleasure by very many people. But he has another profound wish: to write a large prose work, which will be related to his 'sinful' fragmentary poems as an artist's big painting is related to the preliminary sketches for it. This aspiration is mentioned only in his student years — we do not read anything later about his giving it up or about his regretting not achieving it; the wish for an unnoticeable style says nothing about prose. Must this not be because, by the time the second lifelong wish is mentioned, Boris Pasternak has almost finished writing his own large work of prose, the novel *Doctor Zhivago* — that is, in some sense, this very novel is the big prose work that Yurii dreams of writing?

The fact that Zhivago is a poet is mentioned rarely and with the kind of non-emphasis that he himself gives it when he chooses a scientific career in the conviction that poetry cannot be a profession any more than innate cheerfulness or melancholy can. This sounds like an extension of Pasternak's remark in Paris in 1935, to the effect that poetry cannot be discussed at conferences: it is 'simpler' than the things that can be discussed there — it does not submit to being institutionalised in any way. Zhivago is in no way set up or instituted as a poet. Nonetheless, most things are experienced by him in the shape of potential poems, and there are three places in the novel which, without showing him either as poet among poets or as poet among non-poets, do show him writing. Each time he is alone, not defining himself in relation to others, wholly absorbed in work. In Part 9, the first Varykino stay, we have the prose of his diary. In Part 15, in Moscow just before his death, we have his notes on modern poetry. Part 14 gives us, in the second Varykino episode, the novel's sole account of Yurii Zhivago composing poetry. He spends two nights writing.

As in all Pasternak's accounts of poetry writing, importance is given to the local surroundings. Not only the quiet, the frost, the dark and the atmosphere of home, but the quality of the ink in the inkwell, and the kind of handwriting used — all belong to the creative process. It is described in terms that may recall Yurii's response to the October Revolution, which began not at the beginning but in the middle of everything. He has been intently copying out old poems, then working away at old sketches for new ones, when, right in the midst of all that, a change takes place. Suddenly 'the relationship between the forces that govern creation stands on its head', the human individual virtually disappears and, with 'headlong swiftness and power', language itself takes over his work

like the huge rolling of the flow of a river which by its very move-ment moulds the stones of the river-bed and turns the wheels of mills . . . it creates, along its way and in passing, metre and rhyme and a thousand other forms.   (14:8)

This river-like force bringing about changes in everything it touches, randomly, easily and 'in passing', recalls many images earlier in the novel as well as the sentence we quoted from Pasternak's English letter in chapter 1 about a 'moving entireness . . . a passing by, rolling and rushing inspiration, as if reality . . . were composing itself out of numberless variants and versions'. But the sentence following the power-ful image of the river is afflicted with the lameness that must accompany too earnest an attempt to be simple about something very elusive. Possibly, with Vedenyapin's concep-tion of history in mind, trying to explain just how history is made up of creative works, and certainly seeking to justify poetry on the largest possible scale, our author writes, with stammering abstractness, that the poet's work was done for him by

the state of the world's thinking and the state of poetry and of universal thought and what was destined for it in the future, and the next sequential step it was to take in its historical development.

After the hours of writing, Zhivago is 'happy, strong and calm', as never in ordinary life. The poet in ordinary life is validated by the poet at work. Weaknesses there turn out to be strengths here. There, he seemed indecisive, here he yields to strengths that, as it were, make decisions through him. There, 'he felt a pigmy before the enormous hugeness of the future . . . and could do nothing'; here, personal insigni-ficance is a virtue: he is 'no more than a pretext or a pivot' − without which the next step of history could not be taken. There, he accused himself of 'characterlessness', felt a lack of outline; here, the blurring of outlines, the hazy mentality, are a prerequisite of creation, for in the long half-awake day between the two nights of writing

> a preliminary half of the work was being accomplished for him by the sleepy haze which filled him and covered everything around him and enwrapped his thoughts: a generalised diffuseness.   (14:9)

A few pages later this diffuseness, productive of poetry, will be juxtaposed again with the never-hazy Strelnikov. Approaching Varykino, Strelnikov is answering the threat of wolves with his gun; for Yurii those same wolves 'were already not wolves on the snow under the moon, but had become a theme of wolves'. In the work they will reappear as the legendary dragon.

The account of the writing of the poem 'Fable' now shows in technical detail how language takes over from the writer. All he has to do is prepare the right line-length, shortening it from pentameter to tetrameter to trimeter. It is notable that as he does this he progressively wakes up, is at last 'completely awake'. By the time he reaches the three-foot line, everything is happening by itself: objects outline themselves, the horse's step is audible, the rider goes into the distance; and the poet scribbles with feverish haste just to keep up. Pasternak has 'demystified' inspiration without losing any of its amazingness.

Not all poems are in trimeters. But the shortening of the line is an enactment of the clearing away of the rhetorical, which is so much a concern of this book. It epitomises Yurii's, and Pasternak's, belief in the life-giving quality of laconicism. Superfluous words must be thrown out not because they contain untruth but because they block the entry of the truth.

'Fable', about St George and the dragon, is the middle poem of the twenty-five-poem cycle and is the only one whose genesis is described in detail. In form an old Russian folksong, it may obscurely suggest a myth for Zhivago's life, since 'Yurii' is a version of 'George', and maybe Yurii's helplessness in the face of the 'years and centuries' is implied by the poem-hero's sleep.

The other poems variously connect with the prose of the novel, some tenuously, some more strongly. One of them, 'Winter Night', is a focus of interconnectedness as such. It starts:

> Snow fell and fell all over the earth,
> To all its bounds,
> A candle was burning upon the table,
> A candle burning.

The refrain, which occurs eight times, enters Yurii's mind at a clearly defined moment in the narrative. He is on his way to the Sventitskys' Christmas party with Tonya, to whom he has just got engaged, and they are passing the house in Kamerger Street where Lara happens to have called in on Pasha to tell him she is 'always in danger'. Her life is at a powerful meeting-point with his, as is Yurii's with Tonya's, and the candle shining down from window to street marks a crossing-point between the fates of the two couples. Further, Lara's and Yurii's paths are about to cross at the party they are separately travelling towards; and eighteen years later Lara will find Yurii lying dead in that very same room. Still more than these 'crossings of feet, crossings of fate' is held in the symbol of the candle, for it also sums up 'the phenomenon of Christmas in all realms of Russian life' and the thought of writing or painting a Russian 'Adoration of the Magi', like the Flemish ones, with frost and wolves and dark spruce forest. Thus it points to another of Zhivago's poems, 'Christmas Star', which depicts, very visually, a kind of Russian Nativity scene, and which also glances ahead to 'all that came later . . . all the future of galleries and museums . . . all the Christmas trees in the world'. These words link up with Vedenyapin's reflections in Part 2 on the moment when Christ appeared in history, a moment which is 'gratefully spread throughout all cradle songs of mothers and all the picture galleries of the world'. So love poem and Christian poem have the same origin in the poet's life, and both poems are products of a richly elaborated coincidence.

As well as such detailed connections, there are links between the poems and the prose on a larger scale. Like the prose, most of the poems contain descriptions of particular places, and treat persons metonymically. They continue, too, the prose theme of overcoming death, which thus develops from the boy's climbing the grave-mound, at the very beginning, to the Gospel story of death and resurrection, at the very end, in the poem 'Garden of Gethsemane'. Above all, the cycle of poems draws out the religious content of the 'novel in prose'. Seven poems are devoted to Christian subjects ('In Holy Week', 'Christmas Star', 'Miracle', 'Evil Days', the two 'Magdalen' poems, and 'Garden of Gethsemane') while another four combine religious and secular subject-matter. (In 'Hamlet' an actor uses Christ's words for his own predicament, Christian references are important in 'August', the first two stanzas of 'Dawn' are tacitly addressed to Christ, 'Earth' has a subtext of the Last Supper.) All except four of the remaining fourteen poems ('Explanation', 'Wedding', 'Fable', 'Separation') are largely about seasons and weathers. Nevertheless the religious content of the cycle is the more marked in that it is announced in the opening poem and then builds up as the cycle progresses. It develops from the few biblical words in 'Hamlet', through the solitary, religiously explicit 'In Holy Week' and 'August', to the sequence of eight Christian poems that close the cycle, with the last one focusing on the moment ('Let this cup pass') that is central to the first one, at the same time making it a mere moment in the larger, far more affirmative, context. History's energies derive from the story of the life of Christ, said Vedenyapin; nearly all the religious poems here re-tell incidents from that story. As Henry Gifford says, it is a 'story that had not been told in Soviet literature for forty years and Pasternak would seem to be discovering it anew for himself'. Certainly, the concern with Christianity in these poems makes them different from all his previous work, and shows the nature and degree of his confrontation with Soviet ideological orthodoxy.

We have seen that Pasternak was mindful of Rilke's peaceful and subtle prose, and of some of his poetry, while writing *Doctor Zhivago*, but Rilke's poems on Gospel subjects,

such as his 'Ölbaumgarten' and 'Pietà', while they must
to some extent lie behind the writing of the two *Zhivago*
poems called 'Magdalina' and the last poem, 'Garden of
Gethsemane', were no close model for him. These poems of
Rilke's are anti-Christian; Pasternak's — despite moments
reminiscent of Rilke's interpretations, such as the lines: 'The
nocturnal distance seemed a region / Of non-being and
annihilation' — are Christian. I shall turn to 'Garden of
Gethsemane' once again, but shall first look closely at the
three opening poems, taking them as typical of the whole
Zhivago cycle.

In his last short period of writing, Yurii notes that what is
needed is a specifically urban poetry, and that the street noise
of the modern city is like the overture just beginning to be
played in a theatre; the author comments that no such poems
were found amongst his papers, though possibly 'Hamlet'
was written in his spirit. The comment is quite mysterious as,
apart from the setting in the theatre, there is nothing especially urban about 'Hamlet'. An actor has gone on stage and
faces a huge, dark audience as if he is facing his own future
lifetime; he does not want to act the role and, in a pre-eminent
example of 'not making a speech', stands there thinking
about it. Finally he prepares to do it, as there is no way out.

Elsewhere Pasternak has written about Shakespeare's
Hamlet not as procrastinator or hesitator but as one sent by
his father to carry out a task and who sacrifices himself in
order 'to judge his own time and serve a more distant one';
Hamlet 'is a drama of lofty sacrifice'. This interpretation
assimilates Hamlet to Christ through the ideas of mission,
obedience, witness and martyrdom, and surely lies behind the
poem, in which the speaker, presumably acting the part of
Hamlet, uses Christ's words in Gethsemane.

But who is the speaker? The 'I' of the poem is compound:
an actor responsible to the play's director and to the expect-
ant audience; Hamlet, responsible for avenging his father's
murder and, in Pasternak's view, for bearing witness to how
the time is out of joint; and Christ, fulfilling the prophecy to
the bitter end. As well as these three persons we sense the

double author, fictional Zhivago and biographical Pasternak, who, by writing the novel, step out with anguish before a vast invisible public, facing present and future judgement (Czeslaw Milosz has called this 'his Hamlet deed').

In chapter 3 we saw how Pasternak kept returning to the theme of acting. In a poem of 1931 he wrote that if he'd known at his début — in the drama of art? — that 'lines with blood in them' will really kill, that acting is as serious as that and the actor must perish, he would have rejected the whole game at the outset; but he did not know, and so now he is accepting the situation in which 'when feeling dictates the lines / It sends a slave onto the stage / And here art has an end / And there's a breath of earth and fate'. Life and art resolve here into one. But in 'Hamlet' there are two different dramas going on, the one the actor has agreed to play, and 'another'. There is no reconciliation between the two and, instead of emerging into a freeing sense of 'earth and fate', the poem ends with the shouldering of duty and inevitability: a melancholy, effortful beginning to the cycle. Yet the poem is light of tone and very finely balanced. Each stanza begins with one or two lines using theatre vocabulary (the third stanza uses it only in line two), then, with no change of tone, continues with two or three lines about life generally, so that four times the situation of actor facing audience is expanded — mildly, laconically — into that of lonely individual facing contemporary and future world. Though the sparse manner and the sober voice remain unchanged, there is some contrast of diction: the humble yet noble plea of the biblical quotation, 'let this cup pass from me', which is the central line and high point in the poem, contrasts with the wry understatement of a familiar proverb about life's difficulty, in the last line: 'living a life is not [i.e. is more than] crossing a field'.

Perhaps the meaning of the 'other drama' is suggested by the second poem, 'March', which while sharing the rhyme scheme and the trochaic pentameter of 'Hamlet' (the only instance of adjacent poems having the same metre), presents a completely different subject and mood. In place of the 'Hamlet' poem's hard-won mood of acceptance, it expresses

simple happiness and freedom. Instead of the restrained tone
of 'Hamlet', with a sense of the lived past informing every
line, it is full of ecstatic exclamations and conjures up solely
the present, as if everything is just beginning. It is set outdoors and with all doors 'wide open', as against the sense in
'Hamlet' that the universe is enclosed in a theatre. In
'Hamlet' the pronoun 'I' – or 'me' or 'my' – occurs seven
times; in 'March' there is no 'I' at all. It praises the kind of
outdoor work and health that Zhivago enjoyed in Varykino,
and it refers in merry manner to the 'overcoming death' motif
with its assertion that all the renewal and growth of spring
derive from manure.

'In Holy Week', the third poem, again affords a complete
contrast. Little can be translated of this lyrical poem in which
the ecclesiastical words are used as musically, liltingly, as the
words of a folk-lullaby and in which everything, even whirl-
pools and the idea of burial, is described with a sort of affec-
tionate delicacy.

It is set in a town, yet the town appears rural (as is
characteristic of Pasternak's town poems): there are trees, no
traffic, the forest is not far off. Like the dream Yurii has
when ill in Moscow, it is about the period between God's
death and resurrection; it is also about the sleep of the earth
before spring. The most remarkable, and very Pasternakian
thing about this poem is that only indirectly is it about people
in church on Good Friday and Easter Saturday waiting for
the midnight announcement 'Christ is risen'. What it directly
talks about is earth, trees, water, air and the month of March,
in a series of images that relate them, only secondarily, to
people. The bare earth preparing a change of weather is like
the Easter service, the pine trees resemble rows of worship-
pers, trees peer into the church to see the proceedings and
observe the procession when it comes out, even making way
for it; and the main feature of the procession's re-entry into
the church building is that the air goes in with it. The air,
moreover, has two flavours: one from the church, the flavour
of communion bread, the other from the weather, 'Spring's
intoxication'. Finally, even the alms-scatterer is not a person

but is 'March', which only resembles a person and scatters snowflakes. The natural and seasonal surroundings are primary; the people are metonymically guessed at through these. In the penultimate stanza, hymns and psalms are heard, and here the human element does come first, yet, like the singing of 'Eternal Memory' in the novel's first sentence, this human communal action of singing spreads into the natural surroundings, for the expectation of resurrection it contains is given in terms of hope for a 'weather-change'.

'In Holy Week' has a special function in the novel. It fills a gap which has been left subtly empty, by taking us back to Part 10. Of the three sections there, the first (about Galuzina) contains many references to the fact that the time is Holy Week, the week leading up to Easter, while the third (about the party for the recruits) is conspicuously placed in the week after Easter. Where is Easter itself? Its place in the text's time is occupied by an undated meeting full of political speeches, blind loyalty to idols and admiration for violence. 'In Holy Week' concentrates fully on the celebration of Easter, filling this temporal and spiritual absence.

Affinity and resemblance between a place indoors and a place outdoors, so strong a feature of many descriptions and metaphors in *Doctor Zhivago*, occurs in several other poems as well. In 'White Night', what one person is quietly telling another (inside, up at their window) 'so much resembles the sleeping distance'. Much of 'Earth' is constructed on the assertion of such similarities. 'Indian Summer' affirms them especially robustly: the 'laughter and ringing of glass in the house' where women are pickling fruit reverberates outside on the slope of a ravine; and after expressing pity for autumn, life's decline and the world's simplicity, the poem reaffirms that cheerful reflection of inner upon outer:

> Indoors the laughter and domestic hubbub,
> The same hubbub and laughter far off.

Likewise, many poems speak of the wholeness of an image or person or atmosphere: in 'March' the idea of all spring phenomena deriving from the single source; in 'Bad Roads

in Springtime', the nightingale's call is caught by everything
– 'earth and sky, forest and field'; in 'Wind', 'all trees as one
entirety' are swayed by the wind; in 'Separation', the
wholeness of the woman's image is suggested by her being
carried by a wave of the sea; in 'Meeting', 'all your image is
composed / Of a single piece'.

Diverse as the twenty-five poems are in subject, metre and
pattern, they are unified through their simplicity of style and
plainness of story-telling. This is especially noticeable in the
religious poems, where the manner is in part the straightforward rehearsing of a well-known story. 'Garden of
Gethsemane', the last poem, in fact follows the Gospel of
Saint Matthew very closely. But its two last stanzas move into
Pasternak's own imagery.

> You see, the course of the centuries is like a parable
> And can catch fire while in movement –
> In the name of its terrible greatness
> In voluntary torments I shall descend into the grave.
>
> I shall descend into the grave and rise on the third day,
> And, as rafts floating down a river,
> As a convoy of barges, the centuries
> Will float to me for judgement, out of the dark.

'Centuries' is repeated, stressing that our concern is time, not
eternity. But how is their course like a parable? And how does
it catch fire? Is this a reference to Revolution breaking out
like flames in the midst of historical continuity? Or to poetry
suddenly kindled amongst ordinary things? Or to someone's
mind flaring up with an awareness of symbolism? Perhaps all
these, and perhaps the centuries' course is like a parable in
that, simple as it is, we can learn immense things from it: that
is from living in time. Something more unequivocal though
possibly not immediately obvious is that 'its' in the third line
quoted above refers to 'the parable', so that Christ's suffering
is conceived as undertaken 'in the name of the greatness of
the parable'. Our reading of the novel has prepared us for this
lightly made yet enormously significant concluding statement. Our consideration of it will be helped by recalling two
remarks, one from the end of the prose part of the book, one

from near its beginning. On the very last page, Gordon, in the same breath as lamenting the collapse of the ideal into the barbaric, regrets the twentieth century's loss of 'the metaphorical, the figurative'. In Part 2, Vedenyapin told his Tolstoyan visitor that the main thing is not what Christ said but the fact that he spoke in parables. The two remarks point to the same thing and are gathered up in this penultimate stanza. Christ is seen as the bearer of symbolism itself. It is for this that he sacrifices his life — for the fragile, shared awareness that makes it possible to speak in parables. This new emphasis is a vital part of Vedenyapin's 'new understanding of Christianity' and of the message of *Doctor Zhivago*.

It is to be noted that just as the church ceremonies in 'A Holy Week' are described by the poet up to the Saturday evening with everyone waiting for the moment of midnight, the start of Easter Sunday (in Russian the word for Sunday and for Resurrection is one and the same), so 'Garden of Gethsemane' (as also the second 'Magdalen' poem) looks ahead to the Crucifixion and Resurrection but stops just before the event, so that the poems end, as does the prose of the novel, in a mood of intense expectation and hope.

In Tarkovsky's 1966 film *Andrei Rublev* there is a series of episodes from the life of the fifteenth-century icon painter, who witnesses many cruelties and atrocities and, having killed a man to save a girl's life, takes a vow of silence; he is released from it three years later when he witnesses a young boy's achievement in supervising the making of a great bell; at the end the bell is raised, and chimes — a symbol of creation and hope. And here the black and white film suddenly explodes into colour. Now we see icon after icon — details of the icons painted by Rublev after this (possibly true) event: the vivid and subtle reds and greens and, above all, the gold of eternity make a tremendous contrast to the horrors in Rublev's life and yet stem directly from them. Perhaps *Doctor Zhivago* may be compared to this film. The final move from prose into verse is like Tarkovsky's move from black and white into brilliant colour, and the many darknesses and deaths in the prose are likewise transformed in the poetry's affirmation of resurrection.

Guide to further reading

The novel itself

The edition of *Doktor Zhivago* referred to and translated from in the course of this book is the Russian-language publication by Feltrinelli, Milan, 1957 (with same page-numbering as the University of Michigan edition of 1959). Only one English translation of the work is available, though in two versions: *Doctor Zhivago*, translated by Max Hayward and Manya Harari – London, 1958, rpt. 1961, 1984, 1988; New York, 1958, with numerous revisions by the American publisher and with the 'Poems' translated by Bernard Guilbert Guerney; later reprinted with further changes. Several translations of the 'Poems' chapter have been separately published, including Donald Davie's in his book *The Poems of Doctor Zhivago*, Manchester and New York, 1965. My book *Pasternak on Art and Creativity*, Cambridge, 1985, contains about forty pages of selected passages from the novel in my translation.

On the Pasternak affair

Materials on the publishing of the novel, award of the Nobel Prize and subsequent Soviet persecution of Pasternak are collected and introduced by Robert Conquest in *Courage of Genius: The Pasternak Affair*, London 1961.

Critical appraisals of the novel

The last chapter of Helen Muchnic, *From Gorky to Pasternak*, London, 1961, is a good introduction to the novel and its poems, with a sketch of the author's earlier work. Three books have been devoted to *Doctor Zhivago* – the one by Donald Davie, mentioned above, which links poems with narrative; Mary F. and Paul Rowland, *Pasternak's Doctor Zhivago*, London and Amsterdam, 1967, which sets out to 'interpret for the general reader the deeper levels of meaning which lie hidden under the surface story'; and Neil Cornwell, *Pasternak's Novel: Perspectives on 'Doctor Zhivago'*, Keele, 1986, a survey of critics' judgments of the novel and of approaches to it. It is not possible to list here the enormous number of published articles and essays on *Doctor Zhivago*, but those up to 1978 are listed in Munir Sendich, 'Pasternak's Doktor Živago: an International Bibliography of Criticism, 1957–1978', *Bulletin of Bibliography*, vol. 37, no. 3 (July–September 1980). Several debates on the novel have been printed; particularly interesting are the debate between Isaac Deutscher (giving a Marxist view) and Irving Howe, reprinted in *Pasternak*, ed. Donald Davie and Angela Livingstone (see below); and the debate between Lionel Abel (who 'likes' the book but does not 'admire' it) and Nicola Chiaromonte in *Dissent*, vol. 4, no. 4 (Fall, 1958), 338–41 and vol. 6, no. 1 (Winter, 1959), 35–44. (The latter, and the bibliography mentioned above, are the only reference I shall give to works which have not appeared in book form.)

On Pasternak's work generally

There exist two volumes of collected essays on Pasternak. One is Donald Davie and Angela Livingstone, eds., *Pasternak*, Modern Judgments, London, 1969, which includes Tsvetaeva's response to Pasternak's poetry in 1922 and Jakobson's 1935 essay on his early prose (see chapter 6). The other is Victor Erlich, ed., *Pasternak, A collection of Critical Essays*, Twentieth Century Views, Englewood Cliffs, 1978, which contains more studies of the later Pasternak. A good introduction to Pasternak's *oeuvre*, in biographical framework and with two chapters on *Doctor Zhivago*, is Henry Gifford, *Pasternak, A Critical Study*, Cambridge, 1977. A more specialised study is Olga R. Hughes, *The Poetic World of Boris Pasternak*, Princeton and London, 1974. My *Pasternak on Art and Creativity*, though it consists largely of Pasternak's own writings (translated), also offers lengthy commentaries on them. Krystyna Pomorska's *Themes and Variations in Pasternak's Poetics*, Lisse, 1975, includes a chapter on the novel. I shall mention three other accounts of Pasternak's poetry: the chapter on Pasternak in Peter France, *Poets of Modern Russia*, Cambridge, 1982; the relevant chapter in Renato Poggioli, *The Poets of Russia, 1890–1930*, Cambridge, Mass., 1960, and Dale Plank, *Pasternak's Lyric: A Study of Sound and Imagery*, The Hague and Paris, 1966. The last-named assumes some interest in literary theory and in the Russian language.

On Pasternak's life

Pasternak wrote two autobiographies: *A Safe Conduct* was published in 1931; *An Essay in Autobiography* was written some thirty years later (see chapter 3). *A Safe Conduct*, an excellent example of Pasternak's early prose style, is printed in my translation in *Pasternak on Art and Creativity* (see above) as well as, in my earlier translation, in the *Collected Prose* mentioned below. *An Essay in Autobiography*, translated by Manya Harari, London, 1959, also exists as *I Remember: Sketch for an Autobiography*, translated by Max Hayward and Manya Harari, New York, 1960. Considerable insight into Pasternak's life and personality may be gained by reading his correspondence, of which there are now three volumes in English: *Letters to Georgian Friends*, translated by David Magarshack, New York, 1968, Harmondsworth, 1971; *The Correspondence of Boris Pasternak and Olga Freidenberg 1910–1954*, translated by Elliott Mossman and Margaret Wettlin, London, 1982 – this correspondence with his cousin, a classical scholar living in Leningrad, reveals much about life during the Stalin years and the war years; Boris Pasternak, Marina Tsvetayeva and Rainer Maria Rilke, *Letters, Summer 1926*, ed. Yevgeny Pasternak, Yelena Pasternak and Konstantin Azadovsky, translated by Margaret Wettlin and Walter Arndt, New York, 1985, is an absorbing exchange of letters between three poets.

Memoirs worth reading are the short, highly evocative account by Isaiah Berlin of his visits to Pasternak in 1945 and 1956, included in his *Personal Impressions*, London, 1980; Alexander Gladkov, *Meetings with Pasternak*, London, 1977; Olga Ivinskaya, *A Captive of Time, My Years with Pasternak*, London, 1978; and Alexander Pasternak (the poet's brother), *A Vanished Present*, London, 1984.

As for biographies, there are now three, with a fourth shortly due to appear: (1) The literary biography by Henry Gifford mentioned above; (2) Guy de Mallac, *Boris Pasternak, His Life and Art*, Norman, Oklahoma, 1981 (a long, detailed work with numerous photographs); (3) Ronald Hingley, *Pasternak, A Biography*, London, 1983 (shorter and less reverent); (4) Christopher Barnes, *Boris Pasternak, A Literary Life*, Cambridge, 1989.

Other works by Pasternak

Poetry cannot be properly appreciated in translation, so I shall not refer in detail to editions of Pasternak's poetry in English, but will note that it has had many worthy translators, including J. M. Cohen, Donald Davie (see above), Peter France with Jon Stallworthy, Henry Kamen, Eugene Kayden, George Kline, Lydia Pasternak-Slater, George Reavey. As regards his prose, I recommend the stories in Pasternak, *Collected Prose*, ed. Christopher Barnes, New York, 1977 and Boris Pasternak, *The Voice of Prose*, ed. Christopher Barnes, Edinburgh, Vol. I, 1986 (Vol. II expected shortly); as well as the non-fictional pieces collected in my *Pasternak on Art and Creativity*. (The story 'A Tale' has also appeared in English under the title *The Last Summer*, translated by G. Reavey, Harmondsworth, 1959.)

Russia: literature and history

In addition to reading the fictional works mentioned in chapter 1, readers may orient themselves more generally in Russian literature by dipping into D. S. Mirsky, *A History of Russian Literature*, London, 1949, and later editions, and may get an idea of dominant Soviet expectations of literature by scanning *Soviet Writers' Congress 1934: The Debate on Socialist Realism and Modernism in the Soviet Union*, London, 1977; they would also do well to read Edward J. Brown, *Russian Literature since the Revolution* (4th ed.), Cambridge, Mass., 1982; Richard Freeborn, *The Russian Revolutionary Novel*, Cambridge, 1982; and Max Hayward, *Writers in Russia, 1917–78*, London, 1983.

Many have sensed the atmosphere of the 1930s in *Doctor Zhivago* – a moving account of the 1930s as experienced by writers and others is given in the memoirs of Nadezhda Mandelstam: *Hope Against Hope*, Harmondsworth, 1975. For a political, social and ideological history of the whole Soviet period, 1917 to (almost) the present day, Geoffrey Hosking's *A History of the Soviet Union*, London, 1985, is strongly recommended.

Other books from which I have quoted in this volume are as follows: Eric Warner, *Virginia Woolf, The Waves*, Landmarks of World Literature, Cambridge, 1987 (see my p. 12); Avril Pyman, *The Life of Aleksandr Blok*, Oxford, 1980 (pp. 243, 274 and 277 of vol. 2, see my pp. 24 and 25); Lazar Fleishman, *Boris Pasternak v dvadtsatye gody*, Munich, 1980 (p. 15, see my p. 26); Emma Goldman, *My Disillusionment in Russia*, 1925 (pp. 8, 22 and 122f., see my p. 29); Jacqueline de Proyart, *Pasternak*, Paris, 1964 (p. 233, see my p. 63); and the unpublished script of the film *Doctor Zhivago*, seen in the Rare Books Room of the University of Illinois library.